William Bircher

A Drummer-Boy's Diary

Comprising Four Years of Service with the Second Regiment Minnesota...

William Bircher

A Drummer-Boy's Diary
Comprising Four Years of Service with the Second Regiment Minnesota...

ISBN/EAN: 9783337173425

Printed in Europe, USA, Canada, Australia, Japan

Cover: Foto ©ninafisch / pixelio.de

More available books at **www.hansebooks.com**

TO THE

SECOND MINNESOTA REGIMENT,

MINNESOTA VETERAN VOLUNTEERS, AND TO THEIR CHILDREN,

THIS VOLUME

IS AFFECTIONATELY INSCRIBED.

READY FOR THE FRONT.

A DRUMMER-BOY'S DIARY:

COMPRISING

FOUR YEARS OF SERVICE WITH THE SECOND
REGIMENT MINNESOTA VETERAN
VOLUNTEERS,

1861 TO 1865.

BY
WILLIAM BIRCHER.

ST. PAUL, MINN.:
ST. PAUL BOOK AND STATIONERY COMPANY,
1889.

TO THE

SECOND MINNESOTA REGIMENT,

MINNESOTA VETERAN VOLUNTEERS, AND TO THEIR CHILDREN,

THIS VOLUME

IS AFFECTIONATELY INSCRIBED.

PREFACE.

As some apology seems to be necessary for the effort herewith made, to add one more volume to the already overcrowded shelf containing the nation's literature of the great Civil War, it may be well to say a few words in explanation of the following pages. I thought that these sketches of my memoranda of army life, as seen by a boy, would prove enjoyable and profitable to my comrades of the Second Minnesota and their children; and I believed that they might at the same time serve to revive in the minds of the veterans themselves long-forgotten, or but imperfectly-remembered, scenes and experiences in camp and field. It was not my original intention to write a connected story, but rather to give to my old comrades the contents of the diary I kept through our term of service, as I have been urgently pressed by so many old comrades to put it into print. And as no full and complete history of the Second Minnesota Regiment has ever been written, it is hoped that these recollections of one of its humblest members may serve the purpose of recalling to the minds of surviving comrades the stirring scenes through which they passed, as well as keeping alive in coming time the name and memory of the organization which deserved so well of its country during the ever-memorable days of now more than twenty-seven years ago. With these few words of apology and explanation, I herewith place the "Drummer-Boy's Diary" in the hands of my surviving comrades.

The illustrations are from the "Recollections of a Drummer-Boy," by kind permission of Messrs. Ticknor & Co., publishers.

WILLIAM BIRCHER,
Company K.

SOUTH ST. PAUL, 1888.

A DRUMMER-BOY'S DIARY.

"FORT SUMTER, S. C., April 12, 1861, 3.20 A.M.
"SIR,—
"By authority of Brigadier-General Beauregard, commanding the provisional forces of the Confederate States, we have the honor to notify you that he will open the fire of his batteries on Fort Sumter in one hour from this time. We have the honor to be, very respectfully,
"Your obedient servants,
"JAS. CHESNUT,
"*Aide-de-camp.*
"STEPHEN D. LEE,
"*Captain C.S.A., Aide-de-camp.*
"MAJOR ROBERT ANDERSON,
"*United States Army, Commanding Fort Sumter.*"

ALL readers of American history will remember this famous order of General Beauregard to Major Anderson, commander of Fort Sumter, and the firing on Fort Sumter by the Confederates.

Without a doubt this issue was expected. It at least found General Beauregard prepared to keep the appointment of his representatives with sufficient punctuality. The hour went slowly by, and the batteries were silent. Five anxious minutes more were counted, and the dark quiet of the night was yet unbroken; but hardly were another five completed, when the flash and the dull roar of a mortar came from the battery on Sullivan's Island. The unconscious shell went up shrieking and wailing along its fiery curve, and lingering reluctantly before its downward plunge, bursting as it fell directly over the doomed fortress.

No meteor of more direful portent ever lit the sky; for this told surely of the beginning of a civil war, compared to which all civil wars before it were as squabbles in a corner; a war in which millions of men were to be engaged, and which was to scatter ruin and want, not only through the country in which it raged, but across the sea, among two of the most powerful nations of the world; which was to convert half a continent into one great battle-ground, and strew it from east to west with the graves of its citizens, slaughtered to gratify the base ambition and the disappointed pride of a small factious oligarchy who justified themselves in their attempt to destroy, with the monstrous assumption of the right of one man to own and use another as his property; but to the eager neophytes in war who manned the Charleston batteries this shell was merely the signal for the beginning of a bombardment in which they expected to run some risk and to gain much glory, for they knew well their overwhelming superiority, both in numbers and in weight of artillery, and they knew how weary, worn, and wasted were their handful of opponents with anxiety, watching, and lack of food.

They expected, also, that after a few such contests, enough to show the government and the people of the free States that they really meant rebellion, they would attain their purposes, and be in a position to so remodel the map of North America as to secure the perpetuation throughout the larger part of its temperate climes (which was the real object sought by their insurrection) of the political and social predominance of the slave-holding oligarchy; so well had politicians been able to cause the citizens of the republic to misunderstand each other! So well had some of them deceived themselves.

The firing of this signal mortar was fitly committed to the hands of Edmund Ruffin, a Virginian, who had grown gray during his untiring efforts to bring about the struggle which he then began. The depression which followed the bombardment of Fort Sumter was but momentary. It did not last a single day The rebound was instantaneous and tremendous. In spite of four months' warning, the event actually came with all the suddenness of surprise. In fact, it was absolutely necessary to the arousing of the loyal men of the republic from a state of mingled confidence and bewilderment, which had almost the seeming and all the effects of stupor.

It was to these people, pending this mental experience, that President Lincoln addressed a proclamation, dated upon the day of firing on Fort Sumter. That was Sunday, and on Monday morning the President's appeal was distributed by telegraph throughout the country. It set forth that the laws of the United States had been for some time defied in the seven seceded States, by combinations too powerful to be dealt with by the officers of the law. It called out seventy-five thousand of the militia of the several States for the purpose of suppressing those combinations.

Governor Alexander Ramsey, of Minnesota, immediately visited the President and offered the services of one regiment, and the organization was commenced. Willis A. Gorman, a prominent attorney of St. Paul, Minn., received a commission from the governor as colonel, and in April the First Minnesota Regiment was mustered into the service of the United States, and June 14 ordered to Washington, D. C. Soon after the departure of the First Regiment the recruiting for the Second Regiment began, and in July had its quota, and was organized with H. P Van Cleve as colonel, James George as lieutenant-colonel, and Simeon Smith, major; and, after doing post duty in the frontier forts, Ripley, Ridgely, Abercrombie, was, in October, 1861, ordered south to Washington. During this period, of July up to August, I had made several attempts to get into the regiment, but, not being over fifteen years of age, and small in size, was rejected. But Captain J. J. Noah, of Company K, seemed to think that I would make a drummer, as the company was in need of one. I was then taken to the office of Mustering-officer Major Nelson, and, after being questioned very carefully in regard to my age, was not accepted until I should get the consent of my parents.

On the receipt of this decision I immediately walked to St. Paul and broached the subject to my parents, who of course objected, but after seeing that I was determined in my idea of becoming a soldier, my father also took the patriotic fever and we both enlisted in K Company of the Second Regiment, and the happiest day of my life, I think, was when I donned my blue uniform and received my new drum. Now, at last, after so many efforts, I was really a full-fledged drummer, and going South to do and die for my country if need be.

During the months of August and September

we did post duty at Fort Snelling and drilled a great deal of the time. In October we received orders to proceed to Washington to join the army on the Potomac. October 14 we embarked on steamboats and proceeded down the river to St. Paul, where we disembarked at the upper landing and marched through the city. Here we found the streets crowded with people waving their handkerchiefs; the band played, the flags waved, and the boys cheered back, and young men brought their sweethearts in their carriages and fell in line with the dusty procession. Even the old people became much excited. As we passed they gave three cheers for the Union forever, and stood waving their hats after us until we were hid from sight. We found the city ablaze with bunting, and so wrought up with excitement that all thought of work had been given up for that day. As we formed in line and marched down the main street towards the river, the sidewalks were everywhere crowded with people, with boys who wore red, white, and blue neckties, and boys who wore fatigue caps; with girls who carried flags, and girls who carried flowers; with women who waved their handkerchiefs, and old men who waved their walking-sticks, while here and there, as we passed along, at windows and door-ways were faces red with long weeping, for Johnny was off to the war, and maybe mother, sisters, and sweethearts would never see him again. Drawn up in line on the lower levee, awaiting the steamboat from the upper landing, there was scarcely a man, woman, or child in that great crowd around us but had to pass up for a last shake of hands, a last good-by, and a last "God bless you, boys!" And so, amid cheering and hand-shaking and flag-waving, the steamboat came floating down the stream, and we were off, with the band playing the "Star-Spangled Banner." We proceeded down the river to La Crosse, where we were transferred to cars, and on the morning of October 16 we arrived at Chicago, and were quartered in the Wigwam where the convention was held that nominated Lincoln for President. After being supplied with rations—of pork, beans, and coffee—we again proceeded on our way, and arrived at Pittsburg, Pa., where we were received by a delegation of loyal citizens, who escorted us to the Duquesne Gray's Hall. Here we found several tables, the full length of the hall, loaded down with eatables of every description, and were waited on by the most beautiful and patriotic young ladies of the city. The hospitality of these loyal people will long be remembered by the boys and cherished in the memory of Pittsburg. Here our orders were countermanded, and instead of proceeding to Washington we were to go to Kentucky and report to General Buell, commander of the Department of the Ohio. We took transports, and with three lashed together we started on our voyage down the Ohio River. We arrived at Louisville, Ky., on October 19, and disembarked and marched out to the Louisville and Nashville Depot. At 5 P.M. we were loaded on flat cars with rough board benches and taken out to Lebanon Junction, where we went into bivouac for the remainder of the night. During our night's ride it rained continually, and, without any protection from it, we were pretty well soaked. October 20, had tents supplied us, and the officers were getting some kind of order out of chaos. We remained here at this camp (which, by the way, was called Camp Anderson, in honor of Major Anderson, of Sumter fame) three weeks doing guard and picket duty. Then we were ordered to the town of Lebanon, where we continued to drill and become more perfect in the manual of arms, and, of course, did our share of picket and guard duty. Here we found the Ninth Ohio Regiment, which had seen service in West Virginia, and we looked upon them as veterans; also the Fourteenth Ohio, Eighteenth United States Infantry, and scattering companies of unorganized Kentucky troops. Our dress parades every evening were viewed by a great many ladies and gentlemen from the adjoining town, and it had a great effect in making the boys try to do their best, as each man thought that he was the particular object of the many young ladies who were viewing the parade while lying here in camp at Lebanon.

We had rumors of all kinds in regard to the prospect of a battle. One day we heard that Zollicoffer was advancing towards Lebanon and that a battle was expected, while the next brought word that he was still in his intrenchments on the Cumberland; then came a report that he was advancing on General Schoepf, who was fortified at Somerset, watching his movements, and later we heard that he had recrossed the river and was on his way to join General Buckner at Bowling Green. Each story passed current until the next was reported.

Three weeks of camp-life wore away and we received orders to hold ourselves in readiness to march at any moment. We were inspected by General Buell and staff, and on the morning of January 1, 1862, we struck our tents, packed our knapsacks, and, with our company property securely stowed away inside our army wagons, with forty pounds upon our backs, we bade adieu to Lebanon and took the road towards Somerset. The air was clear and warm and the road was in excellent condition, but our knapsacks were a burden to us, and before we marched ten miles we found here and there a man dropping out of the ranks to lighten his burden. Shirts, socks, drawers, and shoes were thrown away to become the lawful property of the first passer-by. We stopped at noon by a small stream to fill our canteens and to eat hard-tack, salt pork, and drink coffee with a relish that nothing but marching could give us.

A half-hour soon slipped around, and then we heard the order "Fall in!" from our colonel, and there was a rush and commotion in the ranks. Knapsacks were quickly slung, and in a very few moments our table was cleared, dishes were packed, and we were marching on again.

We marched until about four o'clock P.M., halting occasionally to fill our canteens and rest a few minutes. After marching twelve miles we turned off the road into an open piece of pasture, the land being skirted on one side by woods and on the other by a small stream, which made it a desirable camp-ground.

A squad of men were detailed to provide wood for the cook, while others went for straw on which to lay our weary bodies to rest.

Now, we thought, the campaign has commenced; we believed there was something to be done. It was no longer in the prospective; we were really going towards the enemy True, there was only a small force of us together,—two regiments of infantry and one battery of artillery,—but we thought that in this movement of a small force there were other movements to be made that would insure us victory.

We had great confidence in ourselves and our generals, and looked forward to the end of our march without a doubt of our complete success.

Our second day's march left the small village of Campbellsville behind us, and here we laid over four days to allow our teams to go back to Lebanon for commissary stores and also to take back some articles with which we could dispense.

Our route thus far had been through rough, hilly country, with but few good farms. From appearances, there was more rain than would supply the wants of agriculture. The land was nobly covered with timber of a very good quality. We also passed many good mill-sites, which in some spots, particularly New England, would be very desirable property. Here they were wholly unimproved, partly from the want of means to erect mills, but mostly from a lack of energy on the part of the settlers. With the right kind of inhabitants and proper laws this might be made a pleasant country, and with the mildness of climate Kentucky might be made to blossom as the rose. It is one of the best-watered countries in the Union. Besides the Ohio River on its northern boundary, the Mississippi on the west, and the Cumberland and Tennessee running through it, it is supplied with numberless small creeks, rivulets, and springs which gush from every hill-side. The land along the streams is very productive and yields large crops of corn and hay The hill-sides, which are too abrupt for cultivation, are covered with timber of the best quality, and the running streams furnish abundant mill-sites for converting it into lumber. Cattle can obtain a good living in the woods all winter, and beef, butter, and cheese readily command good prices. The land is broken. Cultivation is good for the production of fruit, while the climate is particularly adapted to fruit-raising. Notwithstanding all these advantages, settlers along the road were reduced to great straits, sometimes to obtain a bare subsistence. Log houses were the rule, and framed were the exception. School-houses languished and ignorance flourished, and the mass of the people were but tools in the hands of the educated few. There is something seemingly inconsistent in this contrast between the advantages of the country and the real condition of the people. There must have been some powerful agency at work to hold so large a tract of country in a state of nature, as it were, while other States, with poorer soil and a colder climate, had made such rapid advance in wealth and productiveness.

The mind at once finds the cause of this and human slavery readily solves the problem. This domestic institution crippled the energy and crushed out the expansive force of the nature of the people with whom it came in contact.

On the morning of January 7 we struck tents again and resumed our march. While in camp near Campbellsville, we had partly passed from autumn to the wintry weather. For the past three weeks the weather had been very pleasant and bright, clear sky, pleasant sunshine overhead, and dry ground under foot. But now a rainy season had commenced, and the transportation was overladen. Now we marched through mud and water, where before we had dust. We did not experience much difficulty from the mud, however, we had a good turnpike road to travel on. But on January 8 we left the pike and turned off on to a mud road, which was well named, for the mud was unfathomable. Companies F and K built a temporary bridge over a small creek near Columbia, a smart little village forty miles from Lebanon, where we found the Fourteenth Ohio Regiment, under command of Colonel James B. Steedman. We encamped two miles from the river, where we laid over two days, waiting for other troops to join us, as we were now approaching the place where the rebels held a strong position, and it became us to be on our guard. On January 11 we left Camp Columbia, and there was no village between us and the host of the enemy. The mud was so deep that we made but little progress, and halted at two o'clock, but six miles from the place we left in the morning. Short as the distance was, our teams did not reach us until after night had drawn her curtain over the busy world, after which our tents were to be pitched and our suppers cooked. As a consequence, it was late in the evening before we satisfied the wants of the inner man and turned our attention to our outer individual. Here we took a philosophical view of the matter and found that our situation might have been a great deal more uncomfortable than it was, for just beyond the fence was a battery of artillery, whose wagons had not arrived. Therefore they had only hard bread to eat and the cannon for shelter. Having a fellow-feeling in our bosoms for fellow-beings in distress, we made an extra kettle of coffee and shared with them, receiving in exchange the warm, heart-felt thanks of the artillery boys.

On January 10 Company K was ordered into the advance, as advance guard. Sergeant McDonough was told to take ten men and proceed about twenty rods in advance of the company, which was to be about eighty rods in advance of the regiment. I was in his squad, and we were again divided into pairs, and kept watch at every turn of the road, so that, if we saw a force of the enemy, we could immediately let the commander know it, and if a body of the enemy should be in front of us, we could discover them in season to prevent a surprise. We saw no enemy, however, worse than the mud, through which we had to plod our way, and at night we encamped within eight miles of where Zollicoffer had a force stationed to scour the country and collect forage and provisions. We had another rest of two days waiting for the other regiments to come up.

Rain fell incessantly; and when we again struck tents, on the morning of January 15, the mud was deeper than ever, and we had a vague idea of passing the night in the woods, with our wagons containing our tents and provisions—particularly that greatest of soldiers' culinary comforts, our coffee—stalled in a mud-hole miles back. This morning our captain, J. J. Noah, returned to Louisville, Ky., on sick furlough. Several of the boys went with him. Lieutenant W. W. Woodbury assumed command of the company. We made a long march, and at night found ourselves in the wild woods without food or shelter, and a long distance in advance of our wagons, while our pickets were posted within two miles of the enemy. We had had a heavy rain the night before, and it had rained at times as we marched. The woods and leaves were very wet; we had no axes, but must have a fire. Now here was a dilemma. How to get a fire started was a question somewhat extensively debated by squads of interested persons. The night bid fair to be still and cool. Our clothes were quite damp, our socks as wet as they could be, and our feet aching with cold.

Necessity is the mother of invention, and with dull and rusty jack-knives—for there was hardly a good one in the company—we fell to work. It was a long job, and required much patience to hew off the dampened surface, and still more to obtain the necessary amount of shavings to ignite the wet and soggy wood which we could pick up in the woods. When did a man undertake a job in downright earnest that he did not accomplish? and after almost an hour of steady labor, we had a bright blaze leaping and crackling through a generous pile of wood and throwing out a cheering light through the dark woods, while our shivering bodies absorbed the heat with gratitude, which none can appreciate until they have gone through the same exposures. As I lay rolled up in my blanket, and peeping occasionally into the dark background of forest around us, I sought for a while to find a definition of the word comfort, and to find out if there could be a position in which a man could be placed and be utterly miserable. While living at Fort Snelling we grumbled a great deal about the provisions furnished us, when we had quite a lengthy bill of fare, containing not only all the necessaries of life but many that might be counted luxuries. On arriving in Kentucky, and having some of the latter articles cut off, we grumbled again, and thought that we were making our stomachs suffer martyrdom for the good of the cause, but amid all these afflictions we looked forward with dread and dismay to the time when we should begin our march and have nothing but hard-tack, pork, and coffee to eat and drink. This, we thought, was the worst we could endure; but now we would have received our rations of hard-tack and pork thankfully; indeed, we would have taken a deal of trouble upon ourselves to have procured them in any form.

Such is human nature. Man, at times, can be the most unreasonable of animals, and at others the most generous; but his noble intellectual organs and impulses are controlled by the larger one of appetite. When a man is found who can shake off all such trammels and bring his sensual organs under the control of his intellectual ones, he has accomplished a feat as rare as it is commendable. Such were my conclusions as I lay before the fire drying my clothes, for even now, without a supper, I found my situation much more comfortable than it had been before the fire was kindled, and far preferred it to that of the pickets who had no fire and were not allowed to build one. As I lay down to sleep, musing in this way, I worked myself into a state of thankfulness that would not have dishonored the Shepherd of Salisbury Plain, and fell asleep to be awakened only by the hum of life and activity in the morning.

Next day our teams arrived, and the boys were all in good spirits. We unloaded the wagons and got the kettles and made some coffee. After that we heard the order "Fall in!" from our colonel. We filled our haversacks with hard bread and commenced our march with our clothes still wet from the rain. Marched eleven miles, to within eight miles of Somerset.

We encamped in an orchard with a beautiful stream running through it, and it made the best camping-ground we had had in Kentucky. We were in camp at this place two days, Friday and Saturday, and now was the time to stand our guard and picket duty. Saturday night Company A, Captain J. W. Bishop, went on picket, and on Sunday morning, January 19, the rebels, under General Zollicoffer, attacked the Tenth Indiana Regiment, and our regiment was quickly ordered to the scene of action. We marched about one and a half miles, through deep mud

ADVANCING TOWARDS THE FENCE AT MILL SPRINGS.

and rain, to stand support to a battery that was in a field throwing shells at the enemy. In a few minutes our regiment was ordered on to the field of battle. We marched by the right flank, up the main road, then made a left oblique movement, then regimental front, and double-quick time until we met the Tenth Indiana. Falling back—they having run out of ammunition—our regiment charged up to a rail-fence, and here occurred a hand-to-hand conflict, the rebels putting their guns through the fence from one side and our boys from the other. The smoke hung so close to the ground on account of the rain that it was impossible to see each other at times. The Ninth Ohio then made a charge along the rebel left flank and drove them from their front; and then followed one of the worst stampedes, I think, that occurred during the war. The rebels left their commander, General Zollicoffer, and Captain Baily Peyton dead on the field. The rebel loss was 192 killed, 140 wounded, and 140 prisoners. Our loss was 39 killed and 207 wounded. We captured 1200 horses and mules, 100 large wagons, 2000 muskets, and 16 pieces of artillery; also their encampment on the Cumberland River, with all their commissary stores.

Our regiment lost 12 killed and 33 wounded. The dead were taken from the field and buried in one grave at our camp-ground. We marched back to camp from the Cumberland River on the 21st and broke camp on the 22d, taking up our line of march to Somerset, Ky., through mud ten to twelve inches deep. We encamped one and a half miles south of the town, on a barren, bleak hill. The night was fearfully cold, and, as our teams did not arrive, we were compelled to stand by the fire all night to keep from freezing. As we had some coffee in our haversacks, it took but a short time to have a cup of hot coffee, and without anything to eat we felt much more comfortable than before. On the 23d, the weather still cold, we marched to the Cumberland River to a small town named after the river, where there is a saw-mill and a few tenement houses. Here we made a permanent camp, and for a week our bill of fare consisted of corn-meal mush and coffee. The boys were troubled a great deal with dysentery, but after getting meat and bread again they soon recuperated their exhausted energies. After three weeks of weary camp-life we were ordered to Louisville, Ky., and on February 9, 1862, we again broke camp and marched through Somerset, the roads still muddy and the weather cold. If we had not been blessed with plenty of dry fence-rails, I do not know how we could have made ourselves comfortable. We remained at this camp two days waiting for commissary stores. For the last few days we were on quarter rations. While on the march, James H. Huges, of Company K, ruptured himself, and felt very badly the next day. February 11 we resumed our march. February 12 it snowed and made the roads still more tiresome to travel. On the 13th we arrived at Crab Orchard, and the roads were no better; but heard from the farmers along the road that we would soon strike the turnpike. We were now sixty miles from Louisville, and on the 14th we moved forward again, with two inches of snow on the ground and the air fresh and crisp. We marched that day twenty-one miles, and at night were compelled to scrape the snow from the ground to get a place to put up our tents, but we had plenty of straw and wood, and were very comfortably fixed. On the 15th the sky was clear and cloudless, the air a great deal warmer than yesterday, but the little snow that laid on the ground made it very hard marching.

Some one started a report that we were to be put on a forced march, and this day's march seemed to favor it. We marched thirty-one miles, and arrived at Danville, a beautiful little village in the Blue Grass Region of Kentucky, at 5 P.M., and went into camp, where we lay over the 16th to sign for clothing and shoes. On the 17th we broke camp at 6 A.M., and marched steadily until 4.30 in the afternoon, arriving at Lebanon (the village we started from New Year's day), having made twenty-nine miles. Here we left a number of sick and disabled, also all unnecessary baggage, such as dress-coats and overcoats. We lay at this camp with thousands of rumors flying around us, some to the effect that we were to march to Munfordville; another that we were destined on a forced march to Nashville; and each one created more or less excitement. We commenced our march in a terrific rain and thunder storm. The water came down in torrents, and streams of mud and water ran along the turnpike, through which we were compelled to wade and plod our way; and we saw that a soldier's life was not so fine as we as school-boys saw it pictured in our histories. We marched twenty-one miles, and encamped on the Jackson farm, a brother of the Jackson who shot Colonel Ellsworth at Alexandria, Va. A short time before this a few of our boys stopped at this place and asked Jackson for some forage for their mules. His answer was, "Yes, I will give you some forage, you Yankee s—— b——s," and commenced firing upon the boys from his front-door. Sergeant Reed and Charley All, of Company I, had revolvers with them, and they drove the old devil into the house, but did not hit him; but afterwards he was arrested and turned over to the civil authorities, who, of course, sympathizing with the South, acquitted him, and he went South and became a general in the rebel army. We found his smoke-house well filled with choice bacon and hams, and his cellars filled to overflowing with all kinds of vegetables and preserves, of which we helped ourselves to our hearts' content. We found abundance of straw and wood, and here we could say we had a picnic. Our clothes were as damp as they could possibly be, and the prospects for drying them before morning were not very good. The rainy weather did not prevent some of the boys from hunting up the distilleries, of which there were a number in the neighborhood, and they came into the tents at night, singing and as jolly as they could possibly be, with from eight to ten canteens full of apple-jack or whiskey hanging over their shoulders; and from the time of their arrival until daybreak singing and story-telling was the order of the night. With full stomachs and a few sore heads on the following day, we bid adieu to the Jackson farm, and felt as though we had punished him just half enough.

The weather was clear and hot, and as we marched and the hot sun poured down upon our damp clothes, it caused a steam to arise from the regiment as if they were cooking. We marched fifteen miles and went into camp. February 25 we marched into Louisville with all the pomp and splendor of the grandest army that ever existed, knowing that we were the saviors of Kentucky, and, having gone through our first battle, considered ourselves heroes; but what was our surprise, while drawn up in line in front of the United States Hotel, in the presence of a bevy of Kentucky's beautiful and patriotic daughters, when one stepped forward and, in a well-prepared speech, presented our colonel with a beautiful silk flag as a token of their appreciation of our valor and bravery at Mill Springs January 19, 1862. Inscribed on this beautiful banner was as follows: "Mill Springs, January 19, 1862, Second Regiment Minnesota Volunteers. Presented by the loyal ladies of Louisville, Ky." Colonel Van Cleve responded in a few eloquent remarks, and then presented it to Jacobas, our color-bearer, who swore they should never be trailed in the dust. At this the regiment marched off to the tune of "Dixie" to the boat-landing on the Ohio River, where our regiment and the Ninth Ohio embarked on the large low-pressure steamer "Jacob Strader" and lay at the levee until the morning of the 26th, then dropped down to Portland and loaded our mules and wagons. Then commenced our journey down the Ohio to Smithfield, at the mouth of the Cumberland River, up which stream we navigated until we came to Fort Donelson, where General Grant captured Buckner and fought that terrible battle. Here we had a few hours to look over the battlefield.

After a hurried glance at the fort we reembarked and proceeded on our way up the river to Nashville. The water was very high and the country for miles around inundated. Houses, hay-stacks, lumber, logs, and *débris* of all kinds were floating down the river. We observed a barn coming down with fifteen or twenty chickens on the roof, and the foragers of the regiment tried to devise some means to capture them; but infantrymen are poor sailors, so they lost the prize. March 1 we arrived at Nashville, and found that Floyd had destroyed the railroad- and wagon-bridge over the river and all of the commissary stores. The city looked deserted. There were a great many fine buildings, particularly the capitol, a very grand and elegant structure, built entirely of marble. March 2 we marched south of town, and encamped on the Granny White Pike Road. We lay at this camp three weeks. Our regiment at that time numbered six hundred, and we spent all our spare time drilling and learning the manual of arms. A great many of the boys went into town every day on passes, visiting the different places of interest and amusement. On April 1, 1862, we commenced our march southward, and as soon as we had taken up our line of march it commenced to rain, and continued until we arrived at our destination. We were without tents or rubber blankets, and the April rains were cold and chilling. At night we would stand near the fires that we had made from dry fence-rails and try to keep warm, but it was impossible. With the cold rain pouring down in torrents, and nothing to protect us from it, we would very near freeze on one side and cook on the other, and the boys were so tired and fatigued that they would fall asleep standing up. One or two of them did fall into the fire before morning. April 7 we heard cannonading in the distance and knew that it was Grant at Shiloh. We were then apprised that we were on the march to assist him. As the booming of the distant guns came to our ears, we forgot our discomfiture, and the excitement caused the boys to very nearly double-quick time, but with all our hurry and rush, we did not get to the Savannah River until the 8th, one day after the battle. We were here loaded on transports and packed in like sardines with our clothes soaking wet, and the cold wind coming down the river seemed to chill us to the marrow. About noon we arrived at Pittsburg Landing, and what a horrible sight met our gaze. Dead men were lying in the mud, mixed up with sacks of grain and government stores, some lying in the water and others trampled entirely out of sight in the deep mud. This was where the great stampede occurred, and no pen can picture the horrors of this part of the field. We disembarked and marched up the hill to Shiloh church, where we went into bivouac. Having no shelter of any kind, we peeled the bark off the gum-trees, and took half of it and laid it on the ground and crawled under it; a small place, but it sheltered us from the elements. While here I saw the spot where General Albert Sidney Johnston, the commander of the Confederate army, fell, and where he was temporarily buried until his body could be sent through the lines to his friends. The battle-field was strewn with the wreck and carnage of war; caissons, dismounted cannon, and dead artillery-horses and their dead riders were piled up in heaps, and the warm sun caused a stench that was almost unbearable. Here and there we could see where a wounded soldier had been pinned to the ground by a fallen limb of a tree, and the shells setting fire to the dry leaves, the poor fellows had been burned alive to a crisp. No historian can ever depict the horrors of a battle-field. The dead lying in every direction and in every stage of decomposition. Squads of men scattered all over the field digging trenches,

c

rolling the dead in, and covering them up with three or four inches of dirt, only to be washed off by the first rain, leaving the bones to be picked by the buzzards and crows. Such is the terror of war.

 I had frequently seen pictures of battle-fields and had often read about them; but the most terrible scenes of carnage my boyish imagination had ever figured fell far short of the dreadful reality, as I beheld it after the great battle of Shiloh. It was the evening of the 9th of April, 1862, when, at the suggestion of a comrade, we took our way over broken-down fences and fallen timber to look over the battle-field. As we wended our way through the troops lying in our front the scene presented to our view was one for the pencil of a great artist. Scattered irregularly were groups of men discussing the battle and its results, or relating exciting incidents and adventures of the fray. Here one fellow pointing out bullet-holes in his coat or cap, or a great rent in the sleeve of his blouse, made by a flying piece of shell; there a man laughing as he held up his crushed canteen or showed his tobacco-box, with a hole in the lid and a bullet among his fine-cut. Yonder knots of men frying steak and cooking coffee about the fire or making ready for sleep. Before we passed beyond our front line, evidences of the terrible carnage of the battle environed us on all sides; fresh, hastily-dug graves were there with rude head-boards telling the poor fellow's name and regiment; yonder a tree, on whose smooth bark the names of two Confederate generals, who fell here in the gallant charge, had been carved by some thoughtful fellow The trees around about were chipped by the bullets and stripped almost bare by the leaden hail; while a log house near by in the clearing had been so riddled with shot and shell that scarcely a whole shingle was left to its roof.

But sights more fearful awaited us as we stepped out beyond the front line. We picked our way carefully among the fallen timber and down the slope to the scene of the fearful charge. The ground was soaked with recent rains, and the heavy mist which hung like a pall over the field, together with the growing darkness, rendered objects but indistinctly visible and all the more ghastly. As the eye ranged over so much of the field as the shrouding mist would allow us to see, we beheld a scene of destruction, terrible, indeed, if there ever was one in this wide world. Dismounted gun-carriages, shattered caissons, knapsacks, haversacks, muskets, bayonets, and accoutrements scattered over the field in wildest confusion. Horses—poor creatures—dead and dying, and, worse and most awful of all, dead men by the hundreds. Most of the Union soldiers had been buried already, and the pioneers yonder in the mist were busily digging trenches for the poor fellows in gray. As we passed along we stopped to observe how thickly they were lying, here and there, like grass before a scythe in summer time. How firmly some had grasped their guns, with high, defiant look, and how calm were the countenances of others in their last solemn sleep. I sickened of the dreadful sight and begged my comrade to come away, come away. It was too awful to look at any more. Even the rudest and roughest of us were forced to think of the terrible suffering endured in this place and of the sorrow and tears that would be shed among the mountains of the North and the rice-fields of the far-off South.

In the camp above mentioned we remained two days, when our teams arrived with our knapsacks and tents, but we were not to have the pleasure of either, as our regiment was detailed to go on picket. On our return, the next day, we found our tents pitched one mile south of our previous camp, where we remained for four days; then we marched south four miles to a camp called Gravelly Hill. Here we were supplied with water from a spring strongly impregnated with iron, and the boys had a very strong idea that they were improving in health wonderfully while they were using it. After another week of rest we moved forward two miles in a drenching rain, and after preparing our camp were detailed for picket duty, with strict instructions not to build any fires. As the boys' clothes were soaking wet, they were in a sorry plight to be out all night without fire. In the morning we were relieved, and returned to camp, where we found our teams with our camp outfits. Here we were inspected by General W. T. Sherman, our new division commander.

From here we moved camp a half-mile or a mile, then threw up works, stayed a day or two, then advanced eighty to one hundred rods, threw up more works, and thus gradually approached Corinth, Miss. On May 29 we heard heavy explosions in the direction of Corinth, and it was reported that the rebels were evacuating the city, and we advanced into the rebel works and found them evacuated.

The boys felt blue about it, as they had been carrying one hundred rounds of ammunition for the last three weeks, expecting a battle every day. It was a sight to see them unloading themselves and scattering the ammunition over the ground in every direction. As a general and commander we thought Halleck was a failure: to have one of the finest-equipped armies of one hundred thousand surrounding a small, half-starved, half-clad army of forty thousand, and then to let them escape! On May 30, at 9 P.M., we were ordered to the left, towards General Pope, and arrived at 3 A.M. on the 31st, and went into bivouac. Orders were issued to carry two days' rations in our haversacks and to unload all extra ammunition; but this order was unnecessary, as the boys had unloaded without orders the day before. At 9 A.M. we continued our march, and did not halt until 1 A. M., June 1, at a deserted rebel camp. We found a large quantity of flour, which we soon appropriated, and cooked it in every way known to the soldiers' culinary art. We remained here all day and night, and on June 2 we moved south one and a half miles and went into camp, where we remained one week. On the 9th we marched twenty-five miles towards Boonville, passing through two deserted towns called Rienzi and Danville, and went into camp. We remained here three days without tents, but the weather was splendid and tents were useless.

Here we had more rations issued, and received orders to return to Corinth on the 13th, where we arrived after a few days' march, with nothing to mar the monotony of the trip. We remained at Corinth a few days, cleaning up, washing our clothes, and doing all necessary repairing. From there we moved east six miles and went into camp. The men had to dig wells to obtain water, and each company built bake-ovens from clay dug from the wells, and they proved to be a perfect success in every particular. The young apples and peaches were now about large enough to gather for sauce, and the boys took advantage of it. It was laughable to see the different dishes they tried to make, and a few of them became very ill in consequence of overeating. A man named Welsy, of my company, died from the effects of eating too much green fruit. After twelve days of pleasant camp-life we went on a three-days' march to Iuka, Miss., where the celebrated medicinal springs are located. Arrived on June 25, and on the 27th we received our pay in postal currency, the first we had seen. On the night of the 27th we marched six miles east. On June 28 we marched fifteen miles to the Tennessee River. Very hot all day 29th Still very hot. Marched seven miles to Tuscumbia, Ala. Here we saw the largest spring of water on our travels, it being sixty feet across where it poured out of the ground and fifteen feet deep, and as cold as ice-water.

We lay here three weeks doing guard duty and drilling. Fourth of July we spent in the city, and were addressed by Governor Ramsey, Generals Fry, Steedman, and McCook. On July 27 we left Tuscumbia behind us and took up our line of march for Florence, where we remained two days. From here we went to Athens, nine miles distant, arriving at 3 P.M. on the 30th. On the following day, the 31st, we marched sixteen miles and went into camp. It rained all night as if the flood-gates of heaven were open.

August 1: We marched sixteen miles through Rogersville. On August 2 we marched fourteen miles. Our beloved brigade-commander, Robert L. McCook, was waylaid and murdered while riding in his ambulance. Not being well, he took the benefit of the shade of the cover of the ambulance, and a couch to lie upon, and drove in advance of the brigade, when the rebel bushwhackers waylaid and killed him before we could go to his assistance. As a revenge the brigade burnt every house within a radius of two miles on each side of the road, and slaughtered all the stock to be found; and I heard that several suspicious-looking characters had given up their lives also. From here we marched to the small village of Dorchester, Tenn., and from there to Winchester and through the town to Decherd Station, where we remained three days, and then moved camp about one mile farther east, where we found a spring of sparkling, ice-cold water.

Here we remained one week, then broke camp, marched fourteen miles, and laid out in the rain all night. The next day we marched five miles to Pelham Gap. Here we remained three days, and heard news of the Indian massacre in Minnesota. We were then ordered to take as many rations in our haversacks as we could carry, and our teams were to go back to Decherd. We marched from here to a hill on the south side of the Gap and remained three days, then received orders to prepare for a long march. On September 3 we arrived at Manchester, Tenn., and encamped in the fair-grounds. Continued our march next day over dusty roads, with the weather very hot. Our camping-grounds had been very good, with plenty of wood and an abundance of pure spring-water. On September 7 we marched through Murfreesboro', and encamped north of the city one mile. We were now aware that General Buell had been outgeneralled by Bragg, who had an army of fifty thousand men marching towards the Ohio River, and was to make a raid through the Northern States. It would be a race between our army and Bragg's to see which should reach Louisville first. At this camp several of the boys made a charge on a farmer's beehives, and the result was, the soldiers were driven from the field. The appearance of their faces and necks was anything but enviable; one. fellow had both eyes closed. I asked him what ailed him, and his answer was, "Toothache: worst case I ever had."

September 9: We marched five miles and encamped. Passed through a beautiful country; fine roads and beautiful weather. September 10: We marched twenty-three miles. We were now four miles from Nashville. September 11: Marched to Nashville and encamped on the Lebanon Pike. Remained there three days, then moved camp near the large fort, where we remained one week.

There we received orders to leave all surplus baggage and tents, and prepare ourselves for marching orders. September 14 flour was issued to us, but no salt. The boys were in a very ragged condition, as all of the quartermaster's stores were shipped from here before our arrival, they expecting that Bragg would take Nashville before we should reach it. September 15: We marched twenty-one miles out on the Louisville Turnpike. We had no coffee or tea,—using sassafras and pennyroyal as a drink,—and no meat, but plenty of flour, of which we made what the boys called "dough-gods." This was done by mixing flour and water into a dough, wrapping it around their ramrods, and baking it before the fire. This was not very palatable without salt, but as it was all we had, we were of course compelled to eat it. The supply of water was short, the streams along the roads being all dry, also the wells at most of the houses. September 16 we marched twenty-two miles. I had no shoes, so I tore up my shirt and wrapped it around my bleeding feet, they being so sore that I could not march without great pain.

September 17: We marched twenty-one miles to Bowling Green. The dust in the roads was four inches deep, and the clouds that arose were suffocating; but in the afternoon it commenced to rain, which cooled the air a little and turned the dust into mud. Passed through Bowling Green on the 18th, marching nineteen miles to within four miles of Cave City We were now near the Mammoth Cave. The 20th we marched five miles, one mile north of Cave City. September 21 we lay over for a rest, and I supposed our generals were watching Bragg's movements. September 22: Moved back to Cave City. 23d: Marched from Cave City to Bacon Creek. September 24: We marched twenty-four miles to Elizabethtown. September 25: Marched to the mouth of Salt River, where it empties into the Ohio. Here we found the boys all barefooted, and no shoes to be had. My rags were worn out, and I had taken the pocket from my blouse and wrapped it around my feet; but as it was very thin stuff, I did not expect it would last over an hour or so. Here we found a boat-load of provisions, but the captain of the boat, being afraid to land, had anchored out in the river.

The boys lined the bank of the river, and begged him to throw off some pork and hard-tack. Colonel Uline then appeared and told the boys to go back to camp, that rations would soon be issued if they would let the boat land. His orders had the desired effect, and shortly after the boys had dispersed the boat landed, and soon afterwards we were furnished with a bountiful supply of bacon, hard-tack, and coffee, and we ate as only half-famished men can. Only he who has marched in the hot sun ten days, with dough and sassafras-tea as a diet, can realize our condition.

September 26, 9 A.M.: Embarked on steamboats for Louisville, Ky., where we arrived in the afternoon and found the whole population out on the streets to see us and for the second time to give us a royal welcome. Handkerchiefs and flags were waving from every window and rooftop, cheers and huzzas resounded through the air from old men, women, and children, who now looked upon us as their protectors and defenders of their homes. September 27: In camp all day We were again supplied with an abundance of rations. September 28: We had clothing and shoes issued to us, of which we were sorely in need. Remained in camp all day. September 29: Received our first pay since our payment at Iuka, Miss.

October 1: We marched from Louisville and encamped eight miles from Shepherdsville. The country was destitute of water. None was to be had except in pools and puddles along the road, which was very warm and putrid. Weather very hot and the roads dusty October 2: We did not move till 4 P.M., when we broke camp and marched to Shepherdsville, arriving at 9 P.M.

October 3: More clothing issued. Remained in camp all day, and on October 4 we resumed our march over the dusty roads; the weather very hot. Crossed the dry bed of Salt River, and encamped with an abundance of straw and wood, but the usual scarcity of water. Found a puddle where we dipped it up with a spoon and strained it through our dirty, sweaty handkerchiefs. October 5: Passed through Bardstown and Portland, and encamped at Fredericktown.

October 6: Skirmished with the enemy all day; passed through Springfield and encamped at Beachfork's Bridge. Plenty of wood and the first good water for a week. October 7: Marched eight miles. Squads were detailed to hunt water, but all came back discouraged and tired out, having found no water except in one well, and there were a hundred there waiting for a chance to get at it. October 8: Lay in camp in view of the battle-field of Perryville, but were not engaged until 3 P.M., when we were ordered forward to support a battery of artillery who were engaged. We found that it was not the most pleasant place we were ever in, but fortunately we had none killed or wounded. Remained on the field all night, and on the following morning, October 9, we moved a few miles to our right and encamped near plenty of good water.

October 10: Weather very cloudy and threatening rain. We marched southeast all day and passed through the village of Perryville. We had plenty of provisions, and good water, wood, and straw,—everything to make us comfortable. October 11: Cloudy and disagreeable. We heard heavy cannonading towards Crab Orchard. We marched two miles and bivouacked until 9 P.M., then marched three miles and found three burning houses. It was supposed that some of our men, while drunk, set them on fire. We marched until 2 A.M. on the 12th, and went into a temporary camp. At 6 A.M. we moved forward again, making a march of ten miles, and went into camp in a grove of hickory- and walnut-trees; good water and plenty of rations. On the 13th we were ordered to the right of our line, and went into camp in an open field, slightly rolling, making a very picturesque camp. That day we drew three days' rations. I made a note of this, for the reason that I wanted to see if rations would be issued again at the expiration of three days. If not, why not? This ration business had been a serious matter with me. I had known the commissary to issue three days' rations and make them last six. This thing would have to be stopped or the government and I would have some difficulty to settle; and, from all appearances, I think it would have been settled in favor of the government, he being the stronger party, and having the advantage. We took what we could get, and found that grumbling did no good. October 14: We marched very rapidly for some cause. The colonel was back and forth along the line urging the boys forward. We had very few rests; passed through Danville at 9 A.M. and encamped ten miles west of it, in an open field, with wood and water near by. October 15: Marched sixteen miles; passed through Lancaster, two miles from Crab Orchard. We lay at this camp three days. Were inspected on the 18th by Captain Gilbert, called by some General Gilbert.

October 19, at 4 P.M., we marched four miles north of Crab Orchard and went on picket. October 20 we were relieved from picket and marched twenty-one miles, within two miles of Danville, resting but three times during our march. October 21: Marched through Danville and encamped at Taylor's Creek, a short march of sixteen miles. October 22: Got over twenty miles of turnpike, and encamped on the Rolling Fork River; plenty of rails, rations, and water. At this camp we remained until the 29th, the teams going to Lebanon for supplies and tents. We also drew clothing and rations. Marched sixteen miles. October 30: The weather and roads fine. We marched fourteen miles and passed through Campbellsville, encamping eight miles south of the village at the forks of the Green River. October 31: Passed through Greensburg and encamped ten miles beyond. November 1: Marched sixteen miles to Cave City, occupying the same camp-ground we did in September. It seemed as if this part of the country was doomed to be overrun by soldiers, as this was the third time we had been there.

November 2: Marched sixteen miles and encamped in an open field; plenty of water a half-mile distant and plenty of dry rails. The next day we left Bowling Green eighteen miles behind us, and were fortunate enough to have a good camp and plenty of wood and water, where we remained until the 7th, and in the mean time rations, boots, shoes, and overcoats were issued to us. Marched twenty miles, passing through the small village of Franklin, and occupied our old camp-ground in our race north with Bragg. November 8: Marched eight miles and encamped at Mitchellsville Depot. Got our water for cooking out of the water-tank of the Louisville and Nashville Railroad. We remained at this camp three days, drew six days' rations, and received a mail. The boys took advantage of the rest, and all wrote letters home to mothers, friends, and sweethearts. On November 12 we moved forward again, and halted at a tunnel on the Louisville and Nashville Railroad, destroyed by John Morgan, the rebel bushwhacker. Marched twelve miles (this was thirty miles from Nashville). We had a good camp, nicely elevated. On the 13th squads were detailed to work in the tunnel. We remained there ten days, the men employed all the time clearing out the tunnel. The weather was very cold and raw. We heard every day the distant boom of cannon towards Murfreesboro'. At 7.30 P.M., November 23, we again broke camp and marched twelve miles through Gallatin, a small village on the railroad. Encamped three miles south. Marched all night and bivouacked at 1 A.M., November 24, on the bank of the Cumberland River for two hours; at 3 A.M. we moved forward again, stopping at a small village at 7 A.M. to cook breakfast, and at 9 again moved forward. Marched five miles more and countermarched, and encamped one and a half miles from the river. Marched twenty-three miles.

c d   5

November 25: Weather cool and cloudy. We broke camp at 9 A.M., and marched five miles to Cunningham's Ford, on the Cumberland River, and encamped in the woods. The timber in this section of the country seemed to be most all hickory and walnut, and the trees were very large. November 26: Weather cool and clear. Teams went back to Gallatin for commissary stores, and took some of the men who were sick to the general hospital. 27th: We heard cannonading in the direction of Lebanon, Tenn. Weather still bright and clear. 28th: The men chopped wood and had a general cleaning-up in camp. 29th: Mail day. Drew overcoats and clothing. We now found out that we were watching John Morgan; we heretofore had an idea that he was watching us. 30th: Had inspection. We had a terrific rain and wind-storm, and limbs of trees flew through the air to the discomfort of all.

December 1: Cold, cloudy, and windy Nothing transpired worthy of mention. December 2 to 5: Nothing occurred to break the monotony of the camp, except that one of our camp-guards built a fire alongside a hollow tree, and about three o'clock in the morning it burnt through and fell to the earth with a crash, in the stillness of the night making a report like a cannon. Colonel George, hearing it, of course thought the rebels were advancing, and immediately rushed in front of his tent, half-dressed, and with his deep-toned voice shouted, "Fall in! fall in! fall in!" and such a scrambling to find accoutrements and guns to get into line our regiment never experienced before or after.

I was drummer of the guard, and knew nothing of it until the regiment had broken ranks and gone to their quarters, when I was highly complimented by the sergeant of the guard for my watchfulness. In the evening it began to snow.

December 6: Had company drill. Captain Woodbury returned from Minnesota. He had left us very nearly a year before. December 7: We heard that Morgan had captured a brigade of new troops of ours at Hartsville. It caused our colonel to strengthen our picket-line and have the men out every morning at four o'clock in line of battle. We lay here doing guard and picket duty until 10 A.M., December 22, when we marched twenty-three miles through Gallatin again, and encamped at Pilot Knob, where we found the rest of our brigade. December 23: We sent out a forage train and had dress parade. 24th: Called out at 1 A.M. and stood in line until three o'clock, then marched to Gallatin, remaining there two hours; then returned to camp, had breakfast, and, in the afternoon, had dress parade to amuse the boys.

December 25,—Christmas: A gloomy one for us. We had for our dinner a bill of fare consisting of baked beans, coffee, hard-tack, and sow-belly 26th: Remained in camp; all quiet. 27th: Called out at reveille to stack arms on the color line. It rained all day, turning cold at night and remaining so. 28th: Cold and disagreeable; had inspection; heard heavy firing north of us. 29th: Nothing new occurred. Weather fine. December 30: I was ordered to beat long roll at 1 A.M., and remained in position until 10 A.M., expecting a skirmish with the Johnnies. While standing in line the boys suffered a great deal from the cold. The weather was cold, and the inactivity of standing so quiet made us feel the cold much more than if we had been actively engaged. We had new clothing issued to us that day. December 31: Weather clear and warm. Taking advantage of it, the officers had a grand review of the troops and general muster, and the boys looked very well in their new uniforms.

January 1, 1863,—New Year: Cold and disagreeable; about as quiet a New Year's day as I had ever seen. Our New Year's dinner was not so grand as it might have been, but then it could have been a great deal worse. We had plenty of pork, beans, and hard-tack, and the sutler had a large stock of delicacies,

A DRUMMER-BOY'S DIARY. 53

and he who was fortunate enough to possess any money could, of course, enlarge his bill of fare and live more sumptuously

That night I was drummer of the guard, and I had been thinking that this thing was coming pretty often. I got but very few evenings to spend with my comrades of the company, but was compelled to remain with the guard at the guard-house every other night. It would have been much easier if the regiment had had its full amount of drummers, and it would have been much more pleasant; but, as it was, Vandyke and I were the only ones left out of the eleven drummers that left Minnesota in '61, and, of course, had to do the entire guard duty. While sitting in the guard-tent I figured up the miles we had marched in 1862, taken from a daily account I kept, as follows: January, 101 miles; February, 149; March, 52; April, 158; May, 36; June, 129; July, 39; August, 101; September, 258; October, 343; November, 98; December, 29; total, 1493 miles for the year. January 2: Weather pleasant, a clear sky, and warm sunshine; remained at company quarters all day. Very quiet in camp. January 3: Cold rain fell during the night, and a cold, raw wind blew all day. We received the *Nashville Union*, which gave an account of the battle of Murfreesboro'

January 4: Four negroes were captured in

the night committing depredations; were handcuffed and shackled, and placed under guard. The wind was blowing a gale at the rate of one hundred miles an hour. K Company detailed for picket at night. January 5: Weather fine. Had battalion drill. We didn't get many fine days that were not taken advantage of by drilling and dress parade, but then we knew it was all for the best.

January 6: Rained,—were compelled to remain in the tents all day. January 7: Cold, disagreeable, and stormy. K Company on picket at night. Received our first mail for three weeks. January 8: Rain, snow, and hail all together made it more interesting. Such weather as this knocked all the enthusiasm out of trying to be a hero, and the most of us were about sick of the hero business. January 9: Rained all day and night: no wind, but a steady downpour of water. January 10: Still raining, keeping us in the tents most of the time. Could not do much cooking outside, so we had to put up with cold, raw, salt pork, hard-tack, and water.

January 11: Clear and bright. Had general inspection and dress parade. January 12: Weather fine. In order to change the programme of daily events, we had battalion drill and grand review. Received a large mail. January 13: At one o'clock in the morning we struck tents and marched out on the Nashville Pike fifteen miles and encamped in an open field, with plenty of wood and water, a half-mile distant from our former camp. January 14: Marched back to Gallatin. Lay along the roads most of the day, and arrived at camp at twelve o'clock midnight, and pitched tents while the rain and hail were coming down in torrents. January 15: Remained in camp all day.

January 16: Rained and hailed up to 11 A.M., then turned into snow and continued all night, until the morning of the 17th; then it cleared up and the sun came out bright, but with a strong, cold wind. An extra heavy picket was sent out that night, I being detailed as drummer of the guard.

Sunday, January 18: Warm and pleasant. Inspection of arms. Quartermaster issued boots and drawers, and the balance of the day the boys wandered around the woods hunting rabbits and gathering walnuts. January 19: Cold, uncomfortable winds blew all night and continued all day. At 4 A.M. beat the long roll, and thought we were to have a repetition of Mill Springs. This was our first anniversary, and the weather was disagreeable. We stacked arms on the color-line, and broke ranks. January 20: Raining and misty. We were without rations, and again we heard grumbling on all sides about the inefficiency of our general officers in letting us martyrs do without our regular rations a few days. Signed for clothing. January 21: Cold and cloudy. The boys amused themselves by chopping wood, and in the afternoon Colonel Bishop ordered the entire camp policed. January 22: Cloudy and cold. Our regiment sent no pickets out. A large mail arrived at 4 P.M. If there was one thing that the soldier delighted in, it was to watch the regimental postmaster distribute the mail to the first sergeants of the different companies and to eagerly scan each package to see if there was some communication for him from some dear one at home; and if, unfortunately, there was none for him, it was sad to see the look of envy he gave those who were more fortunate and had received papers and letters from home; but after the owner of a paper had got through with it, the entire company would read it.

January 23: Cold, raw wind, but a bright, clear sky. Remained in camp all day. A few of the regiment left for the hospital at Nashville.

Saturday, January 24: Cloudy and cool. We were reviewed by General Rosecrans.

Sunday, January 25: Regimental inspection at 10 A.M. Sent out four companies on picket duty. A darky came into camp and reported that he knew where there was a large quantity of lard buried, and that we should come with him and he would apprise us of its whereabouts. The commanding officers concluded to send out a detail the next day to see what truth there was in his assertions. January 26: Lieutenant-Colonel Bishop, with Companies A, B, F, and I, were sent out with four wagons across the Cumberland River to get the lard the darky reported as being buried; and about 7.30 P.M. they returned with twenty-five barrels, leaving seventy-three barrels at the river bank to be sent to Nashville by flatboat. January 27: The pioneer corps loaded the lard on a barge and took it down the Cumberland River to Nashville. We had a snow-storm that day, but not as heavy as we generally had in Minnesota. January 28: Orders were given to be ready to march at 4 P.M., but were countermanded.

January 29: Bright, clear, and dry, but cold. We were loaded on the cars at Gallatin and went to Nashville, and marched out on the Nashville and Chattanooga Railroad, and found our brigade. January 30: Weather fine. At 12 M. we marched ten miles to Stone River, and encamped on a hill with plenty of wood and water. January 31: Marched six miles and halted, and went into camp, and received orders to be prepared to march all night, but orders were countermanded.

February 1: Rained all day. Marched eleven miles and encamped on the Wilson Pike. February 2: Marched ten miles to Mill Creek and went into camp. Very poor water, but plenty of cedar rails. February 3: In camp all day, brushing and cleaning up. February 4: Four companies went out foraging, and in the afternoon returned with eight wagon-loads of potatoes. From the 5th to the 14th we lay in camp, and about all we did was draw our rations, cook, eat, and do guard duty. February 15: Cloudy. Lieutenant Lovilla H. Holmes, of Company H, with sixteen men, routed a company of rebel cavalry which they met while out foraging. The report in camp was that they killed and wounded sixteen of the rebels, and two of the Company H boys received slight wounds. February 16: K Company went out foraging. Weather in the morning clear and cool, and in the afternoon it commenced to rain, and continued all night. While sitting in the tent, Christian Kersamair, of my company, had been using a twelve-pound elongated shell for an anvil to do some repairing on his knapsack, and, after getting through with it, he gave it a gentle kick and rolled it out of the tent. It rolled down into the fire in front of the tent, and in a few moments an explosion occurred that awoke the whole camp. It scattered the fire in such a shape that it was impossible to find a coal or a stick of the wood that had been there, and, most wonderful to say, no one was hurt. Our tent was covered an inch thick with ashes and dirt, and pieces of the shell flew all over the camp. February 17: Wilbur F Little returned to the regiment from the hospital. Rained all day. From the 18th to March 3 we spent our time in battalion and regimental drill, repairing the bridge over the creek, and washing. That day we broke camp and marched fifteen miles to Triune, Tenn., and captured four rebel officers.

March 4: Skirmished all day Captured sixty-two prisoners and three hundred horses and mules. Marched nine miles. March 5: Marched eighteen miles to Chapel Hill, and drove the rebels out of town. Marched back six miles and encamped on a low flat, with plenty of good water and plenty of wood.

Friday, March 6: Rainy and cloudy Sent teams back for rations. Marched twelve miles and went into camp at Triune. Rations arrived at 10 P M. March 7: Cloudy and rainy. Moved camp back of Triune. Teams came up with tents, and we were soon made comfortable. March 8: Cloudy and cool. Regiment went to work building fortifications. Company K went out foraging. Heavy firing in direction of Harpeth Creek. The regiment was ordered out, but did not get into action. The first East Tennessee Cavalry, Colonel Jim Brownlow, reported rebel cavalry trying to cross the creek, but he, with his regiment, prevented them. Everything quiet up to the 13th, when we were ordered to Harpeth Creek to work on the bridge. Saturday, March 14: Returned to camp. Sunday, March 15: Inspection of arms. Rumor in camp that Vicksburg had surrendered, and that the rebels were marching to reinforce Bragg in our front.

From the 16th to the 25th nothing occurred to enliven us or break the monotony of camp-life, except the arrival of the paymaster on the 19th, which always seemed to lighten our troubles. On the 25th, our regiment and the Ninth Ohio marched out three miles with the expectation of meeting some bands of rebel cavalry who were scouring the country for forage, but were not successful in finding them. 26th: The regiment went out foraging to General Stearns's plantation, and came back with an abundance of corn-fodder and corn. I was compelled to remain in camp all day on account of dysentery, with which I had been suffering for some time. This was the first time that I had been absent from the regiment since I became a member. 27th: Weather pleasant up to 12 M., then commenced to rain and continued all night.

Sent my pay, which amounted to fourteen dollars, to my mother. 28th: Warm and pleasant. We drummed a fellow belonging to the Thirty-fifth Ohio out of camp for theft. 29th: Regiment received new Enfield rifles, and the boys felt that they were better armed than ever. March 30: Light fall of snow, which made it very muddy and disagreeable in camp. March 31: Colonel James George arrived from Minnesota and looked hale and hearty. Teams arrived from Nashville with supplies.

April 1: Went out twelve miles to Harpeth Creek after forage. 2d: Called out at 4 A.M. in line of battle. Marched two miles and returned at 12 M. April 3: Warm and pleasant. Marched sixteen miles to the Murfreesboro' Pike and repaired the road. April 4: Returned to camp.

At Triune, not having any cook, we took turns at cooking. In the mess to which I belonged there was a fellow by the name of Stalcup, who was one of the greatest gormandizers I ever saw; but if there was any one thing he was fonder of than another, it was chicken gizzards. That day it was my turn to cook for the mess. Stalcup "cramped" a big fat chicken, killed it, and then told me to cook it for the boys, but to be sure and save the gizzard for him; and I promised him I would. I dressed the bird, cut it up, and put it into the kettle to cook, but, not being an expert at cooking, I forgot to cut the gizzard open, turn it inside out, and cleanse it from all its foreign substances, but simply put it in whole to cook. At noon I pronounced the dinner ready, and Stalcup was on hand and yearning for his gizzard. He plunged his fork into the dish, and, taking out the gizzard, he opened his monstrous mouth and took it in one mouthful. But shortly afterwards he began to curse like a sea captain, as he spit about half a pint of gravel stones out of his mouth, and said to me, "You're a fine cook, ain't you?" The boys laughed so to see Stalcup take turns at spitting and swearing, that they could hardly eat their dinner. The next time I cook a chicken, you bet, I will not forget to dissect the gizzard.

April 5: Grand review and general muster. Troops made a fine appearance. 6th: Warm and pleasant. Orders to march the following day. 7th: Warm. At 1 A.M. we marched out to Eagleville with the expectation of capturing a regiment of rebels. After surrounding the town we found they had been apprised of our approach and had fled. April 8: We received our band instruments from Cincinnati, Ohio. April 9: Warm and pleasant. We heard heavy cannonading in the direction of Franklin. April 10: Regiment went out to a plantation owned by a rebel named Guinn, and loaded the wagons with hay and corn-fodder.

April 11: Warm until 6 P.M. Commenced to rain and continued through the night. Up to the 15th of the month we had done nothing but drill and guard and picket duty, and during that time it rained off and on every other day. April 16: Regiment went to Nashville to guard a supply train. Encamped near the outskirts of the city. Marvin Emery returned to the regiment that day. April 17: Marched back to camp and signed the pay-roll. April 18: Received four months' pay, amounting to forty-eight dollars. 22d and 23d: Warm and pleasant. Remained in camp all day. 24th: regiment went foraging. Marched sixteen miles. 25th: R. G. Rhoades, of Company E, took the leadership of the band, and practised for the first time. I held the prominent position of snare-drummer. 26th: Company G, which had been doing provost duty in Triune, returned to the regiment. From that time to April 30 we enjoyed camp-life wonderfully, with good health, plenty of rations, and drilling enough to give us an appetite. Nice weather and everything conducive to good health.

May 1: We had the little dog-tents issued to us. They were quite a novelty, and made a wonderful difference in the movement of the army, as each man carried his half of the tent, and it made considerable difference in the number of teams required to haul the large wedge-tents heretofore used. 2d: Had brigade drill, and built arbors over our little tents.

Sunday, May 3: Rain fell in the forenoon; had inspection. 4th to the 14th: Had brigade drill every day and dress parade in the evening, which took up most of our time. During the month of May we worked on the breastworks, and drilled every afternoon, under our new brigade commander, General Brannan.

June 1: Grand review. Marched steadily for three hours. 2d: Went out foraging. Marched twenty-five miles. Sent all of our surplus baggage back to Luverne. Second Brigade joined us. 3d: Drill and dress parade. 4th: Weather fine. During the day had division drill under command of General Granger. During the drill we heard heavy artillery firing in the direction of Franklin, and before we left the drill-ground we had orders to proceed to camp and prepare for marching orders. At 7 P.M., with rain pouring down in torrents and with two days' rations in our haversacks, we started for Franklin. Marched all night through deep mud and in darkness such as we had never seen before. It was impossible to see the men marching in front of us, except when the lightning would flash;

then it would blind us so that it was impossible to see for a few minutes afterwards. Arrived at Franklin at 4 A.M. 5th: Hot. Remained in the road all day, and towards evening we went into camp. 6th: We marched back to Triune, and a more tired lot of boys it would have been hard to find. 7th: Sabbath. Major Burkhardt, of the First East Tennessee Cavalry, was captured, but made his escape, and was back in camp. He said there were a few of the boys still in the hands of the rebels.

From June 8 to the 24th we had one continuous order,—regimental drill in the forenoon, brigade and skirmish drill in the afternoon, and in the evening dress parade. The men had long wished for the campaign to commence, as steady drilling had become very monotonous. We received the order with joy to break camp at 7 A.M. and prepare for an aggressive campaign. With three days' rations in our haversacks, we left Triune and marched south seventeen miles. 25th: Marched all day on the Shelbyville Pike, and skirmished with the Confederates. Our entire march was eleven miles.

June 26: Rainy and disagreeable. Drove the rebels through Hoover's Gap. 27th: Marched twenty miles to the small village of Manchester. Encamped in an abandoned cotton-field. 28th: Warm and pleasant. Marched six miles;

skirmishing in our front all day. 29th: Rainy and disagreeable. Our regiment on the skirmish-line. One of the Company I boys shot a rebel courier who was carrying despatches. After being shot, and knowing that he would be taken prisoner, he tore the despatches into hundreds of small bits, so that it was impossible to put them together again to read. 30th: Lay quietly in camp. Second Brigade skirmishing.

July 1: Hot and sultry. We marched into Tullahoma and captured two hundred prisoners; and at this place the boys were very fortunate to find a large quantity of tobacco, of which they supplied themselves with enough to last them a long time. Marched seven miles.

July 2: Hot and dusty. We marched eight miles and were compelled to fight every inch of our way with our skirmish-line.

July 3: Marched ten miles and crossed Elk River, a wide and very rapid stream. We had no pontoons, and therefore were compelled to stretch a strong rope over the river and use it as a support. With one hand the troops held on to the rope, and with the other held their accoutrements and guns up out of the water. In some places the water was very deep, and, of course, some would go under for a few seconds; but we all arrived safe on the south bank, with our clothes more or less wet. Sandin, one of the band, swam over several times with some of the boys' instruments and the bass drum, and fortunately brought everything over in good shape.

Saturday, July 4: My seventeenth birthday. A salute of one hundred guns was fired,—not on account of my birthday, but the birth of the republic. Marched four miles out on the Hillsboro' Road. 5th: Rainy all day. 6th and 7th: Rumors in camp of the capture of Lee with twenty-five hundred prisoners and one hundred and ten cannon.

July 8: Received the news that General Pemberton had surrendered to Grant on the 4th. His entire army and the city of Vicksburg capitulated. Marched two miles to the front and encamped. On the 17th we received the news of John Morgan's raid into Indiana and Ohio. 18th: We broke camp at 7 A.M. and marched seven miles to Winchester, encamping near a ravine, where there were twenty-five sparkling ice-cold springs that flowed from under the hill, forming a beautiful stream of water. We lay in the shade most of the time, near by, during the heat of the day, and did our reading and writing. 19th: Very hot. Had inspection of arms and dress parade. 20th: Regiment paid off. I received $44.75. 21st: Warm. The sutler had supplied a great many of the boys with liquor, and they were feeling pretty good.

22d: Good news from Ohio. We heard that John Morgan had been captured. 23d and 24th: Very quiet in camp. The band serenaded Colonel Vanderveer, of the Thirty-fifth Ohio, our brigade commander.

July 25: Warm and pleasant. After dress parade we serenaded Lieutenant-Colonel Bishop, who left us on a short leave of absence to return to Minnesota, and our wish was that the trip might be the means of improving his health, as he had worked hard to make the regiment gain the reputation it had. The colonel was regarded as one of the finest disciplinarians in the army, and we therefore felt proud of him and wished him *bon voyage*.

July 26: Had general inspection. Colonel Bishop started north. 27th: Sam Gould, of K Company, a deserter, was brought back to the regiment from Indiana, where he had been found by a United States marshal. We serenaded the Second Minnesota Battery, and were most royally treated by the boys. We lay at Winchester until August 16, putting in our spare time in regimental and brigade drill.

While there we were visited by several clergymen, who held religious services in the different camps, and they were well attended by the men. One, particularly, always drew large crowds, the Rev. Mr. Boynton, of Ohio, the father of Major

Boynton, of the Thirty-fifth Ohio Regiment. We wished he could have stayed with us always, as he was a very good, kind, and pious man, and I thought he would be the means of improving the moral character of our men. After a long spell of camp-life, we again received with joy the order for a forward movement, and on the 16th we broke camp at 4 A.M. and marched five miles and went into camp. We found plenty of corn and vegetables, and the change from our regular government rations to green stuff was very acceptable to the boys.

August 17: Marched five miles and encamped at the foot of the Cumberland Mountains. We had plenty of corn and green beans. 18th: Weather hot. Marched up the mountain six miles and encamped on the site of the Southern Episcopal University Nothing had been built except the foundation, which was very massive, and showed that the structure that was to go on its top was intended to be very grand. Before the war, General Polk, now of the rebel army, was an Episcopal bishop, and for several years had been collecting money in the North to complete this structure.

August 19: Hot and sultry Marched down the mountain sixteen miles into the Sequatchie valley, where we found plenty of peaches, apples, corn, and an abundance of clear, cool water, which we appreciated, as we had had no water since the morning before. 20th: Warm and pleasant. Remained in camp all day. Our diet now consisted mostly of fruit. 21st: Hot and sultry all day. Marched to the Tennessee River, where we went into camp. The rebel pickets were on one side of the river and ours on the other, and they were holding conversation with each other. The general topic was about the war. 22d: Hot and sultry. No rations in camp, and the fruit had all been gathered in that vicinity, so it looked rather dubious. Went out foraging and got a few yams. They did well to fill up on, but had no substance. In a very short time after satisfying our appetites we would feel hungry again. 23d: Went foraging again, and were fortunate enough to find a few apples and sweet-potatoes, and found an Illinois boy who had captured a hog, of which I bought a fore-quarter for thirty-five cents. After arriving in camp my messmates and I had a banquet fit for a king. 24th: Hot and depressing. Heard distant booming of artillery on our right. 25th: Still oppressively hot during the day. We heard the rumbling of cannon in the distance. 26th: News of the fall of Sumter and Wagner reached camp, and the boys felt jubilant. 27th: All quiet on the Tennessee. Teams hauled timber to construct rafts to float the army over the river. Weather a little cooler. 28th: Warm and pleasant. Large crews of men worked on the rafts. 29th: Warm, with a cool breeze. Several of us boys took a stroll up the high mountain in our rear, and after a long and tiresome walk we found ourselves on the summit, and the view that met our gaze was something grand. At our feet stretched for miles away like a thread the Tennessee River, winding its way at the foot of the mountains until it dropped out of sight, as it seemed, into some hidden valley.

August 30: Warm and pleasant. Crossed the Tennessee River on the rafts that the boys had been making during the last few days, and encamped in a dense forest four miles from the Georgia line. 31st: Warm. The boys were all down at the river the most of the day, bathing and washing up their clothes. Our foragers had been very successful. They came in by the dozens, loaded down with sweet-potatoes, pumpkins, and fresh pork. Our teams had as yet not crossed the river.

September 1: Weather pleasant and warm. At 2 P.M. we broke camp and marched three miles south to the foot of the mountains and encamped. We found plenty of forage, such as green corn and sweet-potatoes. We were still near the Tennessee River. We lay here until the morning of the 5th. Orders were issued prohibiting the men from bathing after 10 A.M., as some of the men had been taken sick, and the regimental surgeon said that they had overdone themselves in the water during the hottest part of the day; therefore the order.

September 5: Exceedingly hot and sultry. We marched seven miles to the foot of the Smoky Mountains and encamped in an abandoned cotton-field, and were compelled to go back two miles to Nickerjack Cave to procure water for culinary purposes. This cave is quite a curiosity. At one time the Confederate government had a large crew of negroes working in the cave, digging salt for the use of the Confederacy. 6th: Marched five miles to the top of the mountain, and encamped near the coalpits. In the evening, a wild, reckless fellow, named Baxter, started one of the coal-cars down an inclined track, about a mile long and very steep, and when it got very near where the track started at a level, it ran into an old mule, which had done duty for many years hauling the cars out of the mine, and mangled it horribly. The car flew to pieces, and one of the wheels was found embedded in a jack-pine-tree at a height of twenty-five feet, and the balance of the car was strewn around within a radius of one hundred and fifty feet. 7th: Hot, dusty, and very sultry. Marched twelve miles towards Trenton,

Ga. Heard heavy cannonading in the direction of Chattanooga.

September 8: Weather still remained very hot. The band serenaded General Van Cleve. The general was then in command of a division in Crittenden's corps. The men and officers of our regiment held him in great respect and veneration. The sutler of an Ohio regiment arrived from Huntsville with a large amount of beer, and there was a perfect stream of soldiers going and coming with canteens to have them filled. He was very liberal (the sutler, I mean). He charged the boys fifty cents a quart or a canteenful. There was a certain class who would have paid one dollar, if that had been the price, —although we did not see any drunken men.

September 9: Very hot and dusty. We received orders to march the next day with two days' rations and knapsacks. We were very short of rations. We had not had a bean or any salt pork issued to us for a month, and with those articles cut off from the soldiers' bill of fare life was not worth living, and patriotism and love of country must take second place.

September 10: Weather continued very hot and the roads very dusty. We broke camp at 7 A.M. and marched twelve miles down the Trenton Valley, our advance coming up to the division in the lead. We encamped near a small stream of dirty water. At this point the road leads up the mountain. Our drinking-water had to be procured one mile up the mountain-side.

September 11: Still very hot and sultry, but the nights were cool and refreshing. We marched nine miles along the base of the mountains and encamped in a beautiful piece of timber, where we found plenty of sweet-corn and green beans, of which we made succotash, and we found that, even without pork, it made a very relishable dish for a hungry man.

September 12: With very dusty roads and hot weather we marched twenty-five miles to the position where General Negley's division was engaged with the rebels and was driven back, and were ordered out on a reconnoissance to the front, six miles, and at night returned to camp. Marched that day thirty-seven miles.

Sunday, September 13: Orders were issued to be ready to move at any moment with two days' cooked rations in our haversacks. These orders were unnecessary, as we had nothing to cook. We were fortunate, however, to find, a short distance from camp, an orchard with the trees loaded down with peaches and apples, of which we stripped every tree.

Monday, September 14: We broke camp at 7 A.M. and marched about two miles, when we received orders to return to camp, where we stayed the remainder of the day.

September 15: Hot and sultry. Marched five miles and encamped near a grist-mill, where we remained until the following morning. 16th: Without any excitement we were formed into line and stacked arms, and remained to await the enemy; but at sundown we saw none worse than the heat. We then broke ranks and proceeded to make ourselves comfortable for the night.

September 17: Very hot and sultry The rebel cavalry made a charge on our wagon train, and if our regiment had not been ordered back as soon as it was, they would have captured our entire supply and ammunition train. On our arrival we found a few of the supply wagons plundered, but no serious damage done, their time being too short. 18th: Remained in camp all day until 7 P.M., when we broke camp, and were on the road all night. We marched eight miles. We could plainly see the camp-fires of the rebel army on our right as we marched eastward. The air was cool, and at times, when we stopped, which was very often, we would build fires to warm by, and, the line being so long, we were continually in smoke the whole night, and our eyes felt very sore from the effects of it. 19th: Hot and dusty. At daybreak, as we marched along, we saw troops falling into line on the right of the road; the artillery was unlimbered, the gunners stood to their guns, and every thing had the appearance of a battle. We marched along the rear of the line until we reached the left wing of the army, where we piled up our knapsacks, formed in line, marched to the front, and deployed skirmishers. We advanced but a short distance in the woods, which was a pine forest, before we came upon the rebel skirmish-line. We heard on our right the heavy roll of musketry and the terrible thunder of the artillery, and it came nearer and nearer, until, in less time than it takes to describe it, we were engaged with Bragg's army. The terrible carnage continued at intervals all day. At night we heard, from all over the field, the cry of the wounded for water and help, and the ambulance corps were doing all in their power to bring all the wounded into our lines. The night was cool, with a heavy frost, and the water was very scarce. We lay on our arms all night, and on Sunday, the 20th, the battle was renewed with terrible slaughter on both sides. Towards noon we heard that Chittenden's and McCook's corps, on our right, had been driven back, and all that was left on the field, to hold in check the entire rebel army, was our corps,—Thomas's Fourteenth. We held the enemy back until evening, in spite of his desperate assaults, and after dark

AT CLOSE QUARTERS THE FIRST DAY AT CHICKAMAUGA.

we retired to Rossville. Here General Thomas posted Negley's right, stretching to the Dry Valley Road, Brannan's (our) division in reserve to Reynolds's right and rear, while McCook's corps extended from Dry Valley nearly to Chattanooga Creek. Bragg's army was too tired and too sadly worsted to attempt to follow on the night of the 20th. On the 21st a few straggling shots were directed against our army at Rossville. Thomas felt that he could not hold his position there against the Confederate army Orders were received at 6 P.M. on the 21st, and by seven o'clock the next morning our army was withdrawn, without opposition from the enemy. This ended the battle of Chickamauga. Though retiring from the field, our army had succeeded in shutting the rebels out of Chattanooga.

Our corps fought bravely and retired in good order after having for two days held every position taken, even after the disaster on our right on the 20th. While we held the battle-field we repulsed every assault of the enemy, and withdrew only when our ammunition and supplies had given out, and it had become certain that the field could not be held for another day The solitary advantage which the enemy had to show was his final possession of the battle-field. Our regiment's loss was unknown to me at that time.

An inspection of our company was had on the morning of the 21st, when every man was accounted for.

September 22d: Our band was detailed to the hospital to assist the nurses in taking care of the wounded. We found the different wards filled, and the wounded still coming in. The large business blocks on the main street were used for hospital purposes. We succeeded in keeping the men of our regiment all together on one floor. They occupied five large rooms, and it was heart-rending to see the poor fellows as they were brought in, shot and mangled in every possible way Every few moments we had to take one out who had died, and put him in the dead-house, where he would remain until there was a wagon-load. Then they were wrapped up in their blankets and eight to ten buried in one hole; but after the rush was over, each had a separate grave. We remained at the hospital until September 25, when we were ordered to return to the regiment, which in the mean time had been busily engaged in building breastworks to protect themselves from the enemy's artillery fire. We were very short of rations, with no prospect of an increase.

During my stay in the hospital, which was filled with sick and wounded, some ladies from the North visited them daily, bringing with them

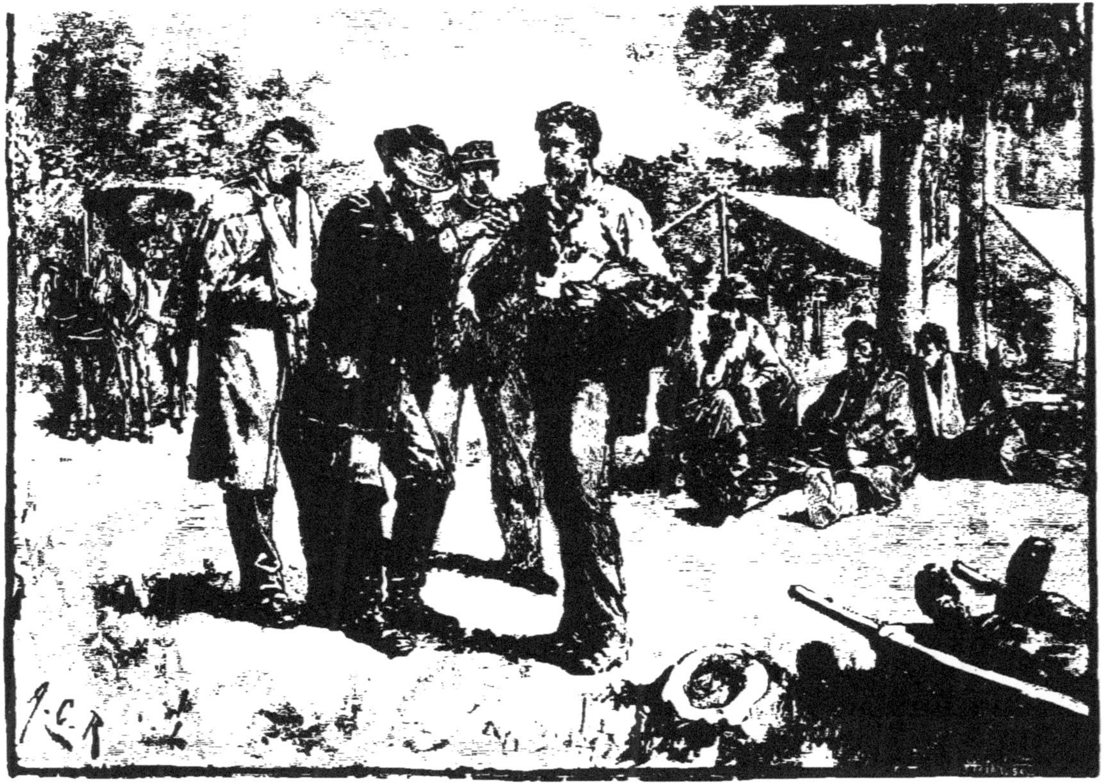

A SCENE IN THE FIELD HOSPITAL.

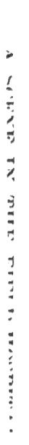

delicacies of every kind, and did all they could to cheer and comfort the suffering. On one occasion, a pretty miss of sixteen, who came down with her mother, was distributing reading-matter and speaking gentle words of encouragement to those around. She overheard a soldier exclaim, "Oh, my Lord!" Stepping up to his bedside to rebuke him for profanity, she remarked, "Didn't I hear you call upon the name of the Lord? I am one of His daughters. Is there anything I can do for you?"

Looking up in her bright face, he replied, "I don't know but what there is." Raising his eyes to hers, and extending his hand, he said, "Please ask Him to make me His son-in-law."

September 26: Regiment worked all day on the intrenchments.

We remained in camp, with nothing to break the monotony of camp-life except the continual firing of the pickets and an occasional shell from the rebel batteries, until Sunday, October 4, when Major Davis left us to return to his home in Maysville, Ky. The major received a slight wound in the head at Chickamauga, and we wished him a safe journey and a speedy return to us, as he was well liked in the regiment.

October 5: Considerable heavy cannonading. Paul Cavitzal, of Company F, was struck in the back with a fragment of shell while lying down behind the works, and we had little hope of his recovery. Up to the 9th there had been every day more or less skirmishing on the picket-line, and the artillery were shelling each other to amuse themselves. There were very few casualties. An election for State officers occurred that day

October 10, 11, 12: Rainy and cloudy. We were out of rations and it looked very blue. We could make ourselves comfortable and protect ourselves from the elements, but to go without our regular rations always threw a gloom over the camp.

I found that an empty stomach caused considerable grumbling and fault-finding, while, if the men had all they wanted to satisfy their appetites, they were generally happy.

Tuesday, October 13: Rained all day Peterson, of Company C, died in the hospital from the effects of a wound received on the picket-line a few days before.

October 14 to the 20th we remained in camp with nothing to create any excitement. We moved back of the general hospitals, and had a high and commanding position and a most excellent camp. From the 20th to the 30th we did nothing but picket and guard duty, and were very short of rations. I was suffering with dysentery, and found that most of the men were in the same condition. We had had no bread of any description for three days.

Saturday, October 31 : The Johnnies on Lookout Mountain tried to shell our camp, but did not succeed in reaching us.

Sunday, November 1 : We had general muster and drill.

November 2: Weather warmer than it had been for some time. The rebs on Lookout Mountain threw a shell, and it passed over our camp and struck one of the hospital buildings, passed through the roof, down between two cots occupied by wounded men, and into the ground, but fortunately did not explode, or it might have been more serious.

On November 3 we (I mean our squad, which consisted of Billy Wagner,—whom we called Jasper Green, for short,—Tibbits, Vandyke, and myself) accomplished a feat which in after years seemed incredible, and I know a great many will doubt it, but, nevertheless, it is a fact.

We were sitting in our tent and talking the matter over in regard to the scarcity of rations, and as we debated the question the conversation drifted to what we would have our mothers cook for us if we were home; and, after mentioning most everything our minds could think of, we had our appetites sharpened up to such a state that our mouths would water every time one of us would give a description of some dainty or toothsome viand. Finally, Jasper, the only one who had any money, offered to go down near the Tennessee River, where the division quartermaster was having some cattle slaughtered for the hospitals, and try to buy some meat.

I procured an order from the regimental surgeon, and, armed with that, Jasper proceeded to get the meat. In the short space of an hour, to our great joy, we espied Jasper at a distance coming with a large chunk of meat on his back, and were still more overjoyed when we found that he had succeeded in procuring twenty-four pounds, which cost him four dollars and eighty cents. We immediately got a large camp-kettle and put in the entire piece, without salt, because we had none, covered it with water, and put it over the fire to boil; and the four of us sat around that kettle and watched until the meat was pronounced done. Now comes the story. We four, half-starved, half-famished men, drank all the broth from that beef and ate every morsel of the meat, without bread or anything as a side dish. I had an idea that some of us would get sick, but I lived over the night to write this in my diary for future reflection.

Gilbert Jackson, of the band, was lying very low at the hospital with diphtheria.

From November 3 to the 15th we had been

on quarter rations, and putting in all of our spare time working on the forts in front of our line.

November 16: Colonel George left us to go back to Minnesota, never to return to us, and the men as a unit were sorry to see him go; but we had Lieutenant-Colonel Bishop in command, and we knew that when he once had entire control of the regiment he would make a model body of men out of it.

November 17: Cold, raw wind and cloudy all day. Regiment went on picket.

November 18 and 19: Cold, cloudy, and disagreeable.

November 20: Great activity in camp. The men were working with double crews on the forts. We had orders to be ready to march the next day at 4 A.M. with one hundred rounds of ammunition. Gilbert Jackson of K Company died.

November 21: Rained all day. The men were still crowding the work on the forts. We noticed that the rebs on Lookout Mountain were also making preparations for an attack.

November 22: Warm and pleasant. We buried Jackson. Had orders to be prepared to march on the morrow with two days' cooked rations and gum blankets.

November 23: We marched at 5 P.M. out to

the picket-line and formed line of battle, and were instructed not to build any fires. The night was very cold, and I, having no stockings or drawers (and I know the boys were all in the same fix), suffered a great deal before daylight.

Tuesday, November 24: Were still in line in front. We could plainly see General Hooker's troops charging up the side of Lookout Mountain. The heavy clouds which all day had enveloped the mountain's summit, and thus to some extent favored Hooker's movements, had gradually settled into the valley, veiling it at times completely from view. Thus the battle of the afternoon was literally "a battle above the clouds." The enemy was repulsed, driven back from the last position where he could make a stand, and hurled over the rocky heights down the valley By this time the darkness upon the mountain rendered farther progress extremely dangerous, and Hooker's troops encamped for the night on the slopes, which they so gallantly won. Lookout Mountain had been captured, and before morning the stars and stripes waved from its peak. The enemy had abandoned his encampment, leaving behind him, in the hurry of his flight, all his camp and garrison equipage.

November 25: Thanksgiving Day. We remained in line until 2 P.M., when we moved to our left one mile and halted to await orders. In the mean time, we took advantage of the time by cooking a kettle of coffee and eating a little lunch, as, from all appearances, we knew that in a short time we would be engaged. At 4 P.M. we were called into line, and Colonel Bishop instructed the line officers that our regiment was to lead the brigade, and that the moment the command was given to advance they should deploy their men as skirmishers, which would save a great many from the enemy's batteries. From the position we occupied we could see every movement of the enemy in the first and second line of works, and they were watching every move we made. We stood in line patiently waiting for the signal to advance. We had not long to wait, however, for at 4.30 P.M., from a signal-gun at Orchard Knob, the entire army moved as one man (our regiment as deployed covering the front of our brigade) towards the first line of works, which we soon reached, and drove the rebels out.

Before we reached the first line of works we crossed an open piece of ground, and as we left our cover of trees and entered this piece of ground the top of the ridge was one sheet of flame and smoke from the enemy's batteries, and the grape tore up the ground around us; but the troops being deployed as they were, there were very few casualties. After taking the first line of works, the troops followed the fleeing rebels up the ridge and charged over the second line of works. Here our regiment captured a rebel battery. After the capture of this line we had but little fighting. The rebel army was routed and fled towards Taylor's Gap in great disorder. We bivouacked on the battle-field for the night, and felt that under General Grant we had regained what we had lost under General Rosecrans. The loss to the regiment was killed, 10; wounded, 9: total, 19.

On the morning of the 26th we gathered arms and accoutrements, piled them up, buried the dead, and marched eight miles south in pursuit of the retreating army of Bragg.

November 27: Marched fifteen miles to Ringgold, Ga. Skirmished all day, capturing twelve pieces of artillery. The Seventh Ohio charged into Taylor's Gap, and their loss was fearful. It was reported that out of fourteen officers they lost six killed and seven wounded.

November 28: Destroyed the railroad track and flour-mill. Weather cold, with sleet and rain. 29th: We marched back to camp, twenty-three miles. 30th: Cold, with wind blowing all day We were still without stockings or underclothing. Had four days' half-rations issued; no crackers.

December 1: We had a grand review. Generals Grant, Thomas, Hunter, and Reynolds, and a score of brigadier-generals were present. After the review Colonel Bishop had inspection of regiment; everything but our clothing was inspected. It was getting to be a serious matter with us. We had not changed clothing for a month or more; and the men were getting filthy and were covered with vermin. We thought that we were accomplishing quite a feat to sustain *ourselves* with the small quantity of rations that were issued to us, without feeding myriads of gray-backs, but we had to remain in this condition until we had clothing issued to us; and when that would occur God only knew.

December 2: Warm and pleasant. Sent some letters home. 3d: Cool and clear; and it made us hug the little fires that we were fortunate enough to find sufficient fuel to build.

December 4: Barnett, of K Company, who was wounded at Missionary Ridge, was buried at 4 P.M. We received the welcome tidings that we were to be supplied with full rations and a supply of clothing in a few days. I went down into the city of Chattanooga and purchased a pair of cotton socks, for which I paid one dollar; one package of envelopes, fifty cents; one package of writing-paper (twenty-four sheets), fifty cents. I saw one of our boys buy a five-pound package of Lynchburg Killikinick smoking tobacco, for which he paid six dollars. Now, comparing this with the then gold basis, he paid fourteen dollars and ten cents for his five pounds of tobacco. I think the government treated us shamefully. They promised to pay us thirteen dollars per month; but we had to pay for everything we bought on a gold basis, which really brought our wages down to a fraction over five dollars a month. The bondholder got his interest and principal in gold,—why should not we? Yes, why not?—that was the question. And another thing that hurt was, that our commanding generals would allow men to come into the lines with goods and charge exorbitant prices for everything they sold,—and still this thing went on. Now there is no question but this thing could have been remedied if it had been looked into by the officers.

December 5: Cold, rainy, and misty. We received a large mail, and of course some papers. We could lie in our tents, under the blankets, and read and pass the time. But we had no rest; the gray-backs kept us moving, and we were compelled to take off our shirts and pants, and sit naked while we skirmished through the above garments and killed all we could find; after which we would have peace for a short time at least.

A very interesting affair occurred that day which furnished considerable amusement to the boys. Wag, or Jasper, in his endeavors to clear his clothes of the pests, caught an unusually large and well-fed gray-back, which he held up between his thumb and forefinger, and said, "I'll bet one hundred dollars that this louse can beat any louse that any man can catch in the tent." About this time I had caught a very large, long, rangy fellow of the razor-back species, who looked as if he had speed in him. So I at once accepted his bet. Now, the question was, how would we get them to run? This matter was soon settled. We took one of our tin plates and held it over the fire until it was very warm, and at a given signal dropped our racers on the hot plate. Wag's jumped the track before he got half way over, and mine went over the entire width of the plate, winning the stakes and the entire gate receipts. This was the first time on record where a gray-back was known to have paid his board. After the race I had a kindly feeling for him, but was compelled to sacrifice him with the rest.

December 7: I and a few of the boys ascended Lookout Mountain, and the scenery from the summit was something grand. It would be impossible for me to give a description of the grandeur, so we will pass it by and leave it for the pencil of the artist. We drew clothing and rations, and to have a warm pair of stockings and good underclothing again made us feel glorious; but we were still on half-rations of meat and coffee. No bread as yet, although we lived in great hopes and faith; but they were poor substitutes for bread.

From December 8 to the 11th there was nothing important occurred in camp, except the regular routine of our daily guard-mount and picket duty.

Our regiment went out to the Chickamauga battle-field to bury the dead, who had lain there for nearly three months. The following rations were issued before we went: half-rations of pork; quarter-rations of coffee and sugar.

December 13: We returned to camp. We heard a great deal of talk of re-enlisting in the veteran service. The recruiting was then in progress.

December 14: A few more of the boys joined the veterans. The thirty days' furlough that was held out as an inducement had the effect to bring in a good many.

December 15: Major Davis returned to the regiment, and appeared to be in excellent health. 16th, 17th, 18th: The recruiting went merrily on. The boys said that if they enlisted and went home, the prospect of starving would be considerably less.

December 19 : I finally concluded that I would re-enlist for another three years. I was still suffering with chronic dysentery, with no hope of getting better if I remained down there; but I thought if I got north, with proper food and good medical attendance, I would recuperate quickly. Crane, of Company F, died that day of dysentery.

December 20 : Company I re-enlisted in a body. The matter of re-enlisting I had considered very seriously, and really thought that I, in justice to myself, should return home, enter some good school, and obtain an education. Having left school for the war at a little over fifteen years of age, my education had since been neglected. At this stage of life I felt the want of an education more than ever. I knew that when the war was ended the country would be flooded with men of the disbanded army, and that a great immigration would soon follow the declaration of peace, and all would want employment; of course I would have to stand my chances with the rest, and with an education I would have an advantage over the common run of wageworkers.

December 21 : The boys were veteranizing fast. It would not be long before there would be enough to be considered a regiment; then there would be an exodus for Minnesota. The weather remained cold and disagreeable and fuel was very scarce. The teams brought wood from the north side of the Tennessee River.

December 22: Company F veteranized to-day. Weather cold. We were again on half-rations. It looked to me as though the powers that be were trying to starve us into re-enlisting.

December 23: Christian Kersemier, of K Company, died of wounds received at Missionary Ridge. The boys in the regiment all remembered the little, short, fat, chunky German, who always carried a very large, well-packed knapsack and a very large haversack, and was never seen without a pipe in his mouth. He received a flesh-wound in the thigh, but he gave up hope, and at last dropped off without a struggle or pain.

Good-by, Christian! You were a good, faithful, and obedient soldier. God will surely give you your reward in heaven.

> "Close around him, hearts of pride;
> Press near him side by side;
> Our Father is not alone.
> For the Holy Right you died,
> And Christ, the crucified,
> Waits to welcome His own."

December 24: All quiet in camp. The re-enlisting continued. The camp reminded one of an old-fashioned political caucus, the way the boys stood around in knots trying to convince others that it was all for the best for them to re-enlist; and some of them, to prove their argument, re-enlisted themselves.

December 25: Christmas: but how dark, how cold and dreary How dismal everything was in camp. The band boys had all re-enlisted except Wagner and I, and we now made up our minds not to remain out; the others had used every endeavor to coax us in, so we at last consented, and were mustered in for another three years.

December 26: A cold, dark, rainy, misty day. We were compelled to remain in the tents all day, under the blankets, to keep comfortable.

December 27: Weather still disagreeable. We tore the floors and the wood-work out of the forts we were so long in building, and used it for fuel. Received a large mail.

December 28: Weather somewhat warmer. The officers were making out our discharge-papers and pay-rolls. 29th: The warmest day we had had for some time. We had full rations of soft bread issued to us. I had always said that once we were re-enlisted there would be an improvement in our rations; and it had come true. The officers were making arrangements for those of the regiment who did not re-enlist. I was told that they would be assigned to the other regiments until our return from Minnesota, when they would again rejoin the regiment and remain until the expiration of their term of service.

December 30: Warm and pleasant. We signed fifteen rolls of every description: some for back bounty, some for clothing, and some for pay. The Ninth Ohio marched to Charleston, Tenn., as an escort to a wagon-train. The Seventy-ninth Pennsylvania Volunteers had dress parade, and the evolutions were all remarkably fine. Our regiment were spectators. Our officers were busily engaged on our muster-out rolls, so we had no parade.

December 31: Cold, cloudy, rainy, and very disagreeable. We patiently waited for our pay and orders to go home, as the time drew near for our departure for the North. It seemed cruel for the boys who had not re-enlisted to be compelled to remain behind, but in a short time they would return home for good.

This being the last day of the year 1863, I figured up the distances of our marches, which amounted to nine hundred and seventy-one miles. The loss in killed and wounded and those who had died of sickness had been heavy that year. One more year of such casualties would wipe the regiment out of existence. My company (K), after the battle of Missionary Ridge, had but six men for duty; not one commissioned officer. The company was in command of Sergeant T.

H. Pendergast, with Corporal Nobles as the only non-commissioned officer to assist, with four privates. The company was then assigned as colorguard, until some better arrangement could be made.

Such are the horrors of war: to-day we are well, hearty, and cheerful, with bright, happy, and fond hopes of a safe return to our homes and families; when the morrow may bring death, desolation, and all the terrors of war upon us, and leave our bones bleaching on some battle-field.

As this was the closing night of the year, we prayed to Him who doeth all things well, our heavenly Father, that this wicked and fearful war might soon end, and the two entire armies be with their dearly loved ones at their peaceful and happy homes.

Friday, January 1, 1864: The weather was very cold. A strong north wind was blowing, which seemed to freeze the marrow in our bones. We were only half clad, having no underclothing; and, there being no wood with which to build fires, we were compelled to be active and on the move all the time to keep warm, or go into the tents and lie between the blankets, which a great many did, and I found it the most comfortable place. It was reported in camp that we were to be paid off on the morrow.

Saturday, January 2: A much more pleasant

day We succeeded in procuring sufficient wood to keep a comfortable fire in the little fireplace in our tent, with Vandyke, Wagner, Tibbits, and I in front of it. Our shivering bodies absorbed all the heat that came from it with gratitude, and we found ourselves much more comfortable than we had been the day before. We did not receive our pay as it had been reported we would. An error in Captain Woodbury's pay-roll was the cause of the delay

January 3: Weather cold and cloudy, with flurries of snow through the day. We received our pay, mine amounting to two hundred and six dollars, father's to one hundred and seventy-nine dollars. At 3 P.M. we were marched in squads to division head-quarters and mustered out of service, and immediately mustered into the veteran volunteer service for three more years. We lay in camp here until the morning of January 8 making preparations for our homeward journey. Our mules had been dying very fast for want of food and of the cold, and the camp was full of sick men suffering with chronic dysentery. As we broke camp that morning and marched to the steamboat landing we hailed the order with joy, knowing that soon we would be in the land of plenty and our suffering would be ended for at least the length of our furlough.

January 8: We embarked on two Tennessee

River steamboats, the "Dunbar" and the "Kingston," and proceeded down the river to Bridgeport, Ala., where we arrived at 3 P.M., and were loaded in box cars, and remained in the yards until 11 P.M. without fire; but here we found a government bakery, where we purchased wheat bread, and therefore did not suffer much from hunger. We rode all night and arrived at Nashville at 12 M., January 9, and marched to the Zollicoffer building, a large block six stories high, which was in an unfinished condition. It was under construction when the war broke out, and its owner took up arms in defence of the South, and was killed at Mill Springs, Ky., and therefore the building remained in the condition he left it.

January 10: At 5 P.M. we moved our quarters to a vacated female seminary, where we found the rest of the regiment, whom we left at Bridgeport, awaiting transportation.

January 11: We received passes for the day to go into the city, where we saw thousands of soldiers on their way home on veteran furlough, and who, like us, were awaiting transportation. Among the novelties we saw here were the ladies, of which we had seen very few since our long and tiresome marches through the South. As they passed us on the streets, we were compelled to stop and gaze after them as if they were fairies.

January 12: We were still in the city awaiting cars. The Fifty-eighth New York Regiment moved into the building we were in, and we found them a very tough lot. They were also on their road home.

Four of our band decided to have what a soldier would call a good square meal. We proceeded to find a restaurant which was capable of filling the bill. After a short time we espied the sign "Donagana Restaurant." Mr. Rhoades, our leader, remarked that the name indicated a first-class establishment, which was, of course, not any too good for us. After a few moments of hurried consultation, we decided to invest in a breakfast, and we also decided that it should consist of fried pork, sausage, potatoes, and buckwheat cakes. In single file we marched into the restaurant and circled around one of the tables. The party consisted of R. G. Rhoades, Chas. Chamberlain, Wm. Wagner, and myself. We took our seats and patiently waited until a waiter should come and take our order. After a few moments a darky came to our table, and the order was given for pork sausage, fried potatoes, and buckwheat cakes for four. The sausages were served on a large platter, and the potatoes and buckwheat cakes in two deep dishes. In less time than it takes me to write it the dishes were empty, and the darky dropped a card in the middle of the table marked "$8.00." Each one of us looked at the other with consternation depicted on our countenances; but Rhoades, not dismayed, ordered the plates refilled, which was soon done. The darky picked up the eight-dollar card and in its place dropped one for fifteen dollars. That broke the camel's back, but not our appetites. We got up from that table with a hungry stomach and a much lighter pocket-book, and I for one shall always keep that name in remembrance,—" Donagana Restaurant."

January 14: We left these quarters and marched to the Louisville and Nashville Depot, where we were loaded into box cars, and proceeded to Louisville, Ky., at 7 P.M. The weather was very cold, and most of the boys were suffering with colds, contracted while sleeping in the houses at Nashville. We arrived at Louisville at 12 M., January 15, and marched to the No. 1 Military Barracks, where we were supplied with pork, hard-tack, and coffee. After supplying the wants of the inner man, part of the regiment was sent to the Soldiers' Home for the night.

January 16: We lay over and the boys were scattered through the city. In the evening a number of the regiment went to the theatre.

January 17: Weather warm and pleasant.

The regiment marched through the streets of Louisville; and I know Colonel Bishop must have felt proud, as the regiment never looked finer nor marched better, nor did the band ever play better, than on this occasion. Every man thought it was his duty to make as splendid an appearance as possible, for we took great pride in our colonel, and he in us. The old veterans had not forgotten the reception we received at the hands of the fair ladies of Louisville in 1862, when they presented us with the beautiful banner that still waved over the regiment as we marched through the streets of that beautiful city. We marched to the ordnance building and turned over our guns and accoutrements preparatory to our departure for home.

Monday, January 18: We crossed the Ohio River to New Albany, Ind., in the morning, and remained in the railroad yards all day. The weather was cold, with snow, sleet, and rain. At 6 P.M. we embarked on cars for Michigan City, Ind. We were fortunate enough to have passenger coaches, something we had not had since we left Chattanooga.

January 19: We were still on the road, sixty miles from New Albany. The railroad company had no wood for fuel, and the water-tanks were all more or less frozen up. The engines died out on the road every twenty-five or thirty miles.

After dragging along at a snail's pace for some time we arrived at Crawfordsville, where we were received by a delegation 'of ladies, who supplied us with coffee and lunch. While here the band was stationed in the depot and discoursed national airs, while the boys ate their lunch and flirted with the young girls. But all good things have an end. The command "Fall in!" was heard, and soon the tall form of Colonel Bishop was seen forming the regiment into position to board the cars, and three cheers were given for the ladies of Crawfordsville. While we were taking our seats in the cars, the ladies on the platform sang "Rally round the flag, boys," which sounded fainter and fainter, until it was drowned to the ear in the noise of the swiftly-rushing train. "Good-by, ladies; may God bless you!"

Thursday, January 21: We arrived at Michigan City, and were transferred to the Chicago road, arriving at Chicago at 6 A.M. on the 22d. Had breakfast at the Soldiers' Home, and immediately proceeded on our journey to La Crosse, Wis., where we arrived at 3 P.M. and were quartered in Turner's Hall. At 9 P.M. we were loaded into covered sleighs, and crossed the Mississippi River on our road to Minnesota. We arrived at Winona at 6 A.M., January 23, and were furnished with a steaming-hot breakfast by the ladies of the place. After breakfast the band performed a few selections, when we again resumed our journey. We passed through all of the little river towns along the road, and everywhere were greeted with great enthusiasm.

We arrived at St. Paul on January 24, and proceeded to the International Hotel, where we were furnished with an elegant dinner, a compliment we, having travelled all day in the cold, heartily appreciated. After dinner I proceeded home to surprise mother, and, as it was dark in the house, she must needs call for a lamp and hold it up close to my face and look me over from head to foot, while she was saying to herself, "God bless you, my boy!" Although I knew that my name had not been forgotten in the evening prayer all the while I was away, yet not once, perhaps, in all that time had mother's voice been so choked in utterance as now, as, with her heart overflowing, she gave thanks for my safe return. When I lay down that night in a clean white bed, for the first time in two and a half years, I thanked God for my safe arrival.

On January 25 the men received their furloughs, and each departed his separate way home, some to see their wives, some their mothers, and others their sweethearts. I hoped that all would receive a hearty welcome, and their stay at home be filled with pleasure and enjoyment. Who could tell, after our return to the South again, who of us would live to come back, and whose bones might remain to bleach on Southern battle-fields?

From January 26 to February 26, the weather had been cold and disagreeable. I had spent my furlough visiting friends in the country and at home with brother Joe, and was again anxious to do military duty. At 9 A.M. I marched to Fort Snelling and reported to Colonel Bishop for duty.

Remained at the fort until the 29th, when we were invited to a banquet and ball at the Winslow House, given by the people of St. Anthony. The regiment marched up in a body, and feasted, sung, and danced all night, and at 7 A.M., March 1, we enjoyed a hearty breakfast, after which we made preparations for our return to the fort. We formed in line with the band playing and the ladies cheering, and amid the many farewells and "God bless you, boys!" we marched back to Fort Snelling. During the 2d we made preparations for our departure to the South.

March 3: Companies I, F, C, G, and K were loaded on common lumber-wagons and proceeded to St. Paul. On our way South, we heard that Charles Chamberlain, our bass-drummer, had broken his leg, and would be compelled to remain in Minnesota for some time.

March 4: Companies D, A, B, E, and H were furnished the same transportation as the rest of the regiment, and also started for the South. The band, with the recruits and head-quarters staff, remained.

March 7: The band and head-quarters staff were loaded in omnibuses, and at St. Paul were transferred to Concord coaches, and proceeded down the river through the towns of Hastings, Redwing, Wabasha, and Reed's Landing. I was so unfortunate as to lose my cap, and was compelled to ride sixty miles bareheaded, the result being a terrible cold.

March 8: We arrived at Winona, and were the guests of the Ladies' Sanitary and Christian Association, who insisted that Colonel Bishop should let the band remain with them over night, to give a concert at the court-house for the benefit of the association. The colonel at first declined, but he could not stand the pleading of so many ladies, so he finally consented, with the understanding that they should take good care of us, and send us along in the morning, all of which they faithfully promised to do, after which the colonel proceeded on his way towards La Crosse. In the evening we gave an instrumental concert at the court-house, which was packed to overflowing. We were quartered in pairs in the finest homes, and taken care of so kindly that the recollection thereof shall always be one of the bright spots in our memory, and we will always say, "God bless the ladies of Winona!"

Wednesday, March 9: We were not fortunate enough to get covered coaches, so we were compelled to take an open conveyance, with a mule and a horse as propelling power, which, with the disagreeable snow and sleet and the muddy roads, made our progress very slow indeed. Another calamity stared us in the face. We should have arrived at La Crosse that night, where we would have been supplied with rations and shelter. Now we were travelling on our own hook, as it were. While the boys had been on furlough they had spent their little money with a lavish hand, and I am not far out of the way when I say the entire party could not have produced ten dollars. The night was cold, and supper and shelter we must have. Arriving at a stage-stopping place, we made our wants known, and explained to the landlord our financial condition. He kindly told us that if we had had money he would not have kept us, but, being in this condition, he would make us a shake-down on the floor and provide food for us, the best he had, and that when we received our first pay we could pay him; all of which we faithfully promised to do.

On March 10, after eating a hearty breakfast and again thanking our kind host, we proceeded on our way to La Crescent, where we arrived at noon. We were again compelled to make known to the landlord our poverty-stricken condition, and, after making him promises of good faith in our intention of paying him, we were told to go into the dining-room and get our dinner, and if we ever thought it worth paying for we could send it to him. He said that in case any of the boys should get killed or die, he would have no claim against their estates. I thought to myself, if that man only knew what a good, honest, kind-hearted lot of boys he had entertained he would never have worried for his pay. The first remark Mr. Rhoades, our leader, made after leaving the house was, "Boys, this man and the one who sheltered us last night shall be paid out of our first month's pay, and I will see that they get it, and I will risk my life on that."

After leaving the hotel, we were told that we could not cross the river, as the ice was moving. Not to be frustrated in our design, we found a couple of boats, but no oars. This was soon remedied. We tore off a few fence-boards, and soon had two sets of oars, after which we embarked in our boats and safely crossed the river to La Crosse, where we found the regiment. Colonel George had joined and taken command. We were quartered in the Westcott House for the few hours we were to remain. A couple of our regiment got into a quarrel, and one of them, named Brown, of Company D, was terribly cut up, and was not expected to live.

March 11: At 3 A.M. we were again put into cars and went as far as Minnesota Junction, where we were unloaded, and remained on the platform of the depot until noon. We then proceeded to Chicago, where we arrived at 7.30 A.M.

March 12: We were quartered in the Soldiers' Home, where we found everything in A No. 1 order, and were furnished with plenty of good food. We remained here until 8 P.M., when we received orders to proceed to the Central Depot. Here we found that the railroad company had made arrangements to send us on South in cattle-cars, but Colonel George remonstrated, and told them they were compelled to furnish first-class accommodations, and that was what he was going to have. Four cars were furnished, and Companies F, K, G, and I, with the band, proceeded on their journey, while the rest of the regiment remained in charge of Captain Donahower, to follow on as soon as proper transportation was furnished.

Sunday, March 13: Lay over at Michigan City to clear away a wreck ahead of us. On Monday, March 14, at 3 A.M., we continued our journey, and arrived at Indianapolis for breakfast at the

Soldiers' Home. After returning to the depot, we found that the railroad company had unloaded our baggage, taken the passenger-coaches away, and supplied us with cattle-cars again. We were compelled to get into them and continue our trip. The band and head-quarters staff were more fortunate. We had a nice coach. We arrived at Louisville at 10 P.M., and were quartered in an old dilapidated rookery without doors or windows, and here we were supposed to make ourselves comfortable.

Through the kindness of Mark Hendricks, a railroad agent, who came through from Minnesota with us, we were furnished a dinner at the United States Hotel.

March 16: Captain Donahower arrived with the rest of the regiment, and were assigned quarters with us. The Sixty-first Ohio Regiment started home on their veteran furlough. We lay here until the 18th, when we again took transportation for Nashville. Arrived at Edgefield at 4 A.M., March 19, and found that the railroad tracks were blocked with trains ready to pull out for the North with troops on their furlough, homeward bound. Seeing that it was impossible to proceed by cars, we disembarked and marched over the river, through Nashville, to the outskirts of the city, and awaited in bivouac while the officers procured quarters for us. At 6

P.M. we marched back into the city and were quartered in a church, where we were very comfortable. We remaind here until March 23, drilling the recruits in the manual of arms and marching. We drew five days' rations and marched out of the city four miles, on the Murfreesboro' Pike, and encamped near a fine spring of icecold water. We found plenty of good cedar rails, and what does a soldier delight in more than to have plenty of cedar rails to build his camp-fires with? We here received our new tents, and felt that we were again in active campaign. I knew that after a few days' marching we would feel better, our appetites would be keener, and we would be more healthful all around.

March 24: Reveille at 5 A.M., and at 7 A.M. we broke camp and marched towards Luverne. Passed through the town, and encamped three miles south. A great many of the recruits were suffering with galled feet. We marched twelve miles and encamped near a clear stream of water, where the boys took advantage of the situation and went in bathing, after which we felt considerably refreshed.

March 25: Weather cloudy, with rain. We marched fourteen miles to Murfreesboro', and encamped on the "Ready" plantation, the owner being the father-in-law of the rebel John Morgan, where there was plenty of wood and water. We found General Van Cleve here looking very hale and hearty.

We remained here until the 28th, when we broke camp and marched twelve miles. The roads were very dusty and the wind blew a hurricane; but towards evening it clouded up and rained a little during the night. 29th: Weather cloudy Roads in good condition. We marched fourteen miles to Shelbyville and encamped on Duck River, on an old rebel campground.

March 30: Weather warm and pleasant. We marched eleven miles and encamped near a beautiful spring, with plenty of wood. We heard that three rebel officers had passed through here northward bound. What their intentions were was a mystery.

March 31: Marched nine and a half miles to Tullahoma and encamped two miles south, where we found plenty of wood and water.

April 1: Cloudy, rainy, and disagreeable. We marched fourteen miles to Decherd. This was a hard day's march. It was not the distance, but the way we were marched. Colonel George made stretches of from four to five miles before he called a rest for the men. They were heavily loaded with all their new clothing and blankets, which made it very tiresome without rest every two or three miles. At the end of the day's march, with the roads in very bad condition in consequence of the rain, the men were all played out.

April 2: Overcast, but pleasant. Marched nine miles over the mountains into Stevenson's Valley. Edmund Garrison, of our regiment, was sent ahead to Chattanooga, he being unable to keep up with the command, having taken sick while marching.

April 3: We marched but a short distance,— five miles. Our teams delayed us. We were now travelling on the railroad track.

April 4: We marched on the track fifteen miles, within one and a half miles of Stevenson, Ala., and went into camp.

April 5: We marched to Stevenson, where we found General Le Duc, of Hastings, Minn., formerly of the First Minnesota Regiment, who had charge of all the military stores there. He informed Mike Allen, of Company I, that if he could get the consent of Colonel George he would give the regiment a barrel of whiskey The colonel gave his consent, with instructions that if a man should get drunk he would be severely punished. With these instructions, Allen returned to Le Duc, who at once had the head knocked out of a barrel and distributed the whiskey to the boys. Very few of them showed any signs of intoxication. After a short stay with General Le Duc, we continued our march, arriving at Chattanooga at 10 P.M., and were quartered in the Soldiers' Home for the night.

April 6: We had breakfast at the Home, after which we marched out to Chattanooga Creek. We drew clothing and a complete supply of camp equipage and rations. General Brannan made the camp a visit, and congratulated us on our safe arrival to the front again. We remained at this camp until the 9th, when we marched out on the Ringgold Road, and passed over the Missionary Ridge battle-ground. Encamped on Chickamauga Creek in a cedar grove.

April 10: We marched nine miles to Ringgold, Ga., where we found those of our regiment who had not re-enlisted. The troops seemed to be in good spirits, and were ready for active service.

April 11: Weather pleasant and warm all day. We worked on our tents and policed the camp-ground. At 6 P.M. we had our first dress parade for three months. The Thirty-fifth Ohio Band serenaded our officers after parade, and invited them over to the court-house to a minstrel show they were giving every night. K. D. Chase, one of the band-boys, was taken very ill that day, and we hoped for his speedy recovery, as he was too good a boy to lose or lie sick long.

April 12: Overcast and rainy; remained in camp all day.

April 13: Warm and pleasant. Martin Smith returned from Minnesota, where he had been lying sick with the smallpox. We remained in this camp until May 6, drilling and doing guard duty. We had been out on several reconnoissances, but with no results. Now things looked as though there was something to be done.

May 7: With three days' rations in our haversacks and three in our wagons, we marched eastward six miles. The Fourth Corps had been skirmishing with the rebels all day. 8th: exceedingly hot. We advanced one mile, reformed our line, and faced in a different direction,—more towards Buzzards' Roost.

May 9: We moved our line more to the right. Skirmished with the rebels all day, until it became so dark that both sides withdrew for the night. The Confederates had a very strong position on the high bluffs on each side of the pass.

May 10: Weather rainy and disagreeable. The advance was still skirmishing with the rebs. During the night they had taken several pieces of artillery up on the mountain, with which they were making it very interesting for our boys.

May 11: Weather overcast and very windy. We remained in camp all day. Had orders to be prepared to march next morning at three o'clock with the utmost care and as little noise as possible.

May 12: We marched according to orders to Snake Creek Gap, a distance of twenty miles, where we found McPherson heavily intrenched. The roads were in a deplorable condition, but after getting into the Gap they were much better.

May 13: We received orders to leave our knapsacks and prepare for a forced march. We heard heavy cannonading in the direction of Buzzards' Roost.

May 14: Cannonading still continued to the east of us. We started at 5 A.M., but after marching a short distance we halted and remained over night. On the morning of May 15 we formed line of battle.

May 16: Warm and pleasant. The rebels evacuated Buzzards' Roost. Our men captured five hundred wagons and all of the rebel killed and wounded. Our division moved through to Calhoun, towards Resaca.

May 17: Marched twenty-five miles. 18th: Weather fine. Marched seven miles through Adairsville. The country we passed through was very fine, and many fine homes were to be seen along our route.

May 19: Weather hot. Passed through Kingston, Ga., a beautiful and picturesque little village. Drove the rebels four miles south of town, where they made a stand. Marched thirteen miles.

May 20: Hot and sultry Report in camp that the enemy were advancing on us from the southeast, but it turned out to be General R. W. Johnson's division of our corps.

May 21: The Ninth Ohio returned home, having served their three years, and were to be mustered out of the service. The separation was a sad one, as the Ninth and our regiment had been together for nearly three years. We had stood shoulder to shoulder in all of our battles and skirmishes, marched together day and night, suffered all the hardships together, and shared the pleasures alike; and now to separate forever seemed impossible. Nevertheless, it was true. We wished them God speed, and that they might live long to enjoy the fruits of their battles and marches.

May 22: Very hot and dusty. We marched twelve miles southwest; forded the Etowah River. It was a laughable sight to see the boys slip on the boulders at the bottom of the river and go under, and get such a ducking that everything they had would be soaking wet. Nothing more serious than a good wetting occurred to any of them. There were a great many stragglers that day; more than on any previous day's march.

May 24: Still very hot. The army marched at daybreak. Our brigade was left to guard the supply train. Colonel Bishop issued strict orders that no person should leave camp under any consideration, or severe punishment was in store for them.

May 25: Still in camp. During the day the weather was hot, but at 5 P.M. it commenced to rain and continued all night. We heard heavy cannonading in front.

May 26: Overcast but pleasant. We marched all day over a very hilly country, and were compelled to assist the teams with the wagons up the hills. We stopped at noon to cook dinner and feed the teams, after which we proceeded on our march. We accomplished a great deal of work, but little marching. We made but ten miles.

May 27: Very hot. We remained in camp until one o'clock, then moved camp one mile. I had the painful experience of being stung by a scorpion. I really suffered more from fright than from the sting. Billy Wagner, whom we called "Jasper Green," took considerable pains to get all the fun out of it he could. After going into camp, Jasper had just finished a "dough-god," and was preparing to sit down on the ground to eat it. Suddenly we heard a scream, and on looking in the direction it came from, we saw Jasper holding up his hand with a scorpion hanging to it. Now came my turn to laugh. I informed Jasper that a scorpion was never known to live long after stinging a Dutchman, and my assertion proved true; and I hope he had considerable consolation from it. The dry leaves were full of the venomous little devils. We did not sleep much at night on account of them.

May 28: We marched two miles south to guard a train. We encamped in an open field. Heavy skirmishing in front.

May 29: We marched back to the rear five miles. A general change of all the line. 30th to 31st: Weather hot. Remained in camp.

June 1: Hot. Marched to the front and encamped. Heavy firing on the skirmish-line. 2d: Rainy all day. Were placed in position in line of battle and commenced to build breastworks. Worked all night. 3d: Cloudy. Balls flying over camp from the picket-line. 4th: Cloudy and rainy all day The rebs tried to drive our pickets in but did not succeed. Two boys of the One Hundred and Thirteenth Ohio, of the Second Division, were wounded.

June 5: The enemy evacuated their works and moved to our left. A Company C boy was wounded and captured. 6th: Weather very hot, —in fact, the hottest we ever experienced. We marched northeast all day, and made but four miles,—a mistake of General Palmer's. 7th: Very hot in the fore part of the day In the afternoon we had a refreshing shower. Moved camp half a mile. Rumor in camp that General Lee had re-enforced General Johnston with fifty thousand men. 8th: Cloudy and rainy. We remained in camp all day. Chas. Chamberlain, of F Company, was sent back to Bridgeport, Ala., to relieve Sergeant A. H. Reed, of K Company, who had charge of the regimental property. Chamberlain's leg gave him a great deal of trouble, and he was not able to walk. 9th: In camp. 10th: Cloudy and rainy. Marched four miles. Found the enemy intrenching very rapidly. Our artillery played on them most of the afternoon. Formed line of battle and encamped for the night.

June 11: Disagreeable and rainy Marched two miles and remained five hours. Moved at 3 P.M. one mile to the right and encamped.

June 12: Rainy and cloudy. Remained in camp all day. The front line built breastworks. Digging becomes almost an instinct with the experienced soldier. It was surprising how rapidly men in the field threw up fortifications, how the work progressed, and what immense results were accomplished by a body of troops in a single night. Two armies would fight in the open field one evening, and by the next morning both would be strongly intrenched behind rifle-pits and breastworks, which it would cost either side much blood to storm and take. If spades and picks were not at hand when there was need of fortifications, bayonets, tin-cups, plates, and even jack-knives were pressed into service until better tools arrived; and every man worked like a beaver.

June 13: Weather clearing up. If we had good weather, we would be far in advance in our movements. 14th: Warm and pleasant. Advanced half a mile towards Kenesaw Mountain and built works.

June 15: Advanced another mile and built more earthworks. We had a rumor in camp that Lieutenant-General Polk, C.S.A., had been killed in front of our corps. 16th: Rebels massed on our front, but our artillery did such effective work among them that they soon fell back in disorder. A rebel deserter confirmed the statement of the death of General Polk.

June 17: Cloudy. Advanced one mile and built breastworks in an open field, in open sight of the enemy. The mud in the fields was six inches deep. Lieutenant Jones, of Company B, was killed. 19th: Rainy and disagreeable. M. V Barber, of K Company, was shot through the bowels, and Lieutenant Rutherford, of F Company, was shot in the arm while the regiment was moving to the right to take a new position.

June 20: The artillery on both sides were keeping up a continuous roar. Our boys, with about forty pieces in our front, were centring the fire on Kenesaw Mountain, and the Johnnies were making us keep behind our works also. A shell, which was thrown from the top of Kenesaw, dropped about two feet from Tom McGuire's tent, of Company D, while he was inside sleeping. It worked its way underneath him and exploded, throwing him and tent eight or ten feet in the air. Strange to say, Tom was more scared than hurt.

June 22: Weather very hot. The rebs shelled our camp all day, but fortunately no one was hurt. In the evening we had orders to move to the right. The night being clear and not a cloud in the sky, and a full moon shining, it would have been very easy for the rebels on Kenesaw to see the glistening of our guns as we marched in the rear of our works. So Colonel Bishop gave orders to carry the gun-barrels down and under the overcoats or blankets, and to make no noise. We thus made the march of nearly a mile right under the guns of Kenesaw in silence and safety. But the commander of the troops we were to relieve made so much noise in getting his men awake and into line as to attract the enemy's attention, and he opened a big gun on us while standing exposed and waiting for the breastworks to be vacated. The flash of the gun was like the full moon, and an instant later the big shell burst at the head of the regiment and killed our sergeant-major and terribly wounded four other men of Company F,—Thornton Harris, Ainsworth, Laviscount, and Mattin. Colonel Bishop promptly advanced the regiment into the breastworks while the troops relieved got out of the way without any more ceremony. Sergeant-Major Wheeler was one of the non-veterans, and had he lived three hours longer would have gone with the others to the rear for his discharge. The enemy kept up the cannonade for several hours, but did not injure any more men in our regiment.

June 23: Colonel George and our seventy non-veterans left us for Chattanooga, where they were mustered out, their three years having expired.

June 24: We heard very heavy artillery firing from both sides, but we were so well protected by our works that we had no casualties.

June 25: One of our shells struck a rebel caisson on our front and exploded it. At the sight of this, our boys sent up cheer after cheer, until the rebels drove us under cover again. From June 25 until July 3 we lay in the works in front of Kenesaw Mountain, and during this time there had been an unceasing roar of artillery. Davis's division charged Clearborn's division of the rebel army, with heavy loss. The weather had been very hot for two weeks. We received eighty-four drafted men from Minnesota. On July 3 the Confederates evacuated their works in our front, and as soon as it was discovered we were ordered in pursuit. We followed them eight miles, and on July 4 were ordered back to Marietta as provost guard. We marched five miles and encamped on Ex-Governor McDonald's place. This was the eighteenth anniversary of my birthday We remained at this camp until the morning of July 13, when we returned to the division in front of Atlanta.

July 14: In camp and everything quiet. We received another batch of ninety-eight conscripts. The weather was fearfully hot.

July 15: We marched back to Marietta and went into camp in a grove of locust-trees in the heart of the city. 16th: General Bishop took command of the post, and Colonel Uline acted as provost marshal. We were living very well, with plenty of rations, and the country was full of blackberries. It was Frederick the Great, I believe, who said that "an army, like a serpent, goes on its belly," which was but another way of saying that, if you want men to fight well you must feed them well. Of provisions Uncle Sam usually gave us a sufficiency, but the table had little variety and fewer delicacies. On first entering the service the drawing of our rations was not a small undertaking, for there were nearly a hundred of us in the company, and it took a considerable weight of bread and pork to feed a hundred hungry stomachs. But after we had been in the field a year or two the call, " Fall in for your hardtack !" was leisurely responded to by only about a dozen men,—lean, sinewy, hungry-looking fellows, each with his haversack in hand. They would squat around a gum blanket, spread on the ground, on which was a small heap of sugar, another of coffee, another of rice, maybe, which the corporal was dealing out by successive spoonfuls. They held open their little black bags to receive their portion, while near by lay a small piece of pork or beef, or possibly a small amount of desiccated vegetables. Much depended, of course, on the cooking of the provisions furnished us. At first we tried a company cook, but we soon learned the saying of Miles Standish,—"If you wish a thing to be done well you must do it yourself; if not, you must leave it to others." This applies to cooking quite as well as to courting. We, therefore, soon dispensed with our cook, although scarcely any of us knew how to cook as much as a cup of coffee. When we took the field, a keen appetite, aided by that "necessity" which is ever the mother of invention, soon taught us how to make bean soup and hard-tack,—prepared "hard-tack." It is a question I have much debated with myself, while writing this diary, whether this chapter should not be entitled "hard-tack," as this article of diet was the grand staff of life to the boys in blue. It would seem that but little could be said of the culinary art in camp without involving some mention of hard-tack at almost every turn. If you take a hard-tack in your hand, you will find it somewhat heavier than an ordinary biscuit, but if you will reduce it to a fine powder you will find that it will absorb considerably more water than an equal weight of wheat flour; showing that in making hard-tack the chief object in view was to stow away the greatest amount of nourishment in the smallest amount of space. I also observed that hard-tack was very hard. This I attributed to its great age, for there was a common belief among the boys that our hard-tack had been baked long before the beginning of the Christian era. This opinion was based upon the fact that the letters "B.C." were stamped on many, if not, indeed, all the cracker-boxes. To be sure, there were some wiseacres who shook their heads and maintained that these mysterious letters were the initials of the name of some army contractor or inspector of supplies; but the belief was widespread and deep-seated that they were without a doubt intended to set forth the era in which our bread had been baked.

Our hard-tack were very hard. We could scarcely break them with our teeth. Some we could scarcely fracture with our fist. Still, as I have said, there was an immense amount of nourishment stowed away in them, as we soon discovered when once we had learned the secret of getting at it. It required some experience and no little hunger to enable one to appreciate hard-tack rightly, and it demanded no small amount of inventive genius to understand how to cook hard-tack as they ought to be cooked. If I remember correctly, in our section of the army we had fifteen different ways of preparing them. In other parts, I understood, they had discovered one or two ways more, but with us fifteen was the limit of the culinary art. When this article of diet was on board, on the march they were usually not cooked at all, but eaten in the raw state. In order, however, to make them somewhat more palatable, a thin slice of nice fat pork was cut down and laid on the cracker, and a spoonful of good brown sugar put on top of the pork, and we had a dish fit for a soldier. Of course, the pork was raw and had just come out of the pickle. When we halted for coffee we sometimes had fricasseed hard-tack, prepared by toasting them before the hot coals, thus making them soft and spongy.

If there was time for frying, we either dropped them into the fat in the dry state and did them brown to a turn, or soaked them in cold water and then fried them, or pounded them to a powder, mixed this with boiled rice, and made griddle-cakes and honey,—minus the honey.

When, as was generally the case on a march, our hard-tack was broken into small pieces in our haversacks, we soaked these in water and fried them in pork fat, stirring well and seasoning with salt and pepper, thus making what was commonly called a "hell-fired stew." But the great triumph of the culinary art in camp, to my mind, was "hard-tack pudding." This was made by placing the biscuit in a stout canvas bag, and pounding bag and contents with a club on a log until the biscuits were reduced to a fine powder; then we added a little wheat flour, if we had it, —the more the better,—and made a stiff dough, which we next rolled out on a cracker-box lid, like a pie-crust; then we covered this all over with a preparation of stewed dried apples, dropping in here and there a raisin or two just for "Auld Lang Syne's" sake, rolled and wrapped it in a cloth, boiled it for an hour or so, and ate it with wine sauce. The wine was usually omitted and hunger inserted in its stead. Thus we saw what truly vast and unsuspected possibilities resided in this innocent-looking, three and a half inch square hard-tack. Three made a meal and nine were a ration, and this was what fought the battles for the Union.

The army hard-tack had but one rival, and that was the army bean,—a small, white, roundish soup-bean. It was quite innocent-looking, as was its inseparable companion, the hard-tack, and, like it, was possessed of possibilities which the uninitiated would never suspect.

It was not so plastic an edible as the hard-tack; nor susceptible of so wide a range of use, but the one great dish which might be made of it was so pre-eminently excellent that it threw "Hell fired stew" and "Hard-tack pudding" quite into the shade. This was baked beans. No doubt bean-soup is very good, as it is also very common. But, oh, baked beans! I had heard of the dish before, but never had remotely imagined what toothsome delights lurked in the recesses of a camp-kettle of beans, baked after the orthodox, backwoods fashion, until one day Bill Hunter, of K Company, whose home was in the lumber regions, where the dish had no doubt been first invented, said to me, "Come around to our tent to-morrow morning; we're going to have baked beans for breakfast. If you will walk around to the lower end of our company tent street with me, I will show you how we bake beans up in the country I came from."

It was about three o'clock in the afternoon, and the boys were already busy. They had an enormous camp-kettle about two-thirds full of parboiled beans. Near by they had dug a hole in the ground about three feet square and two deep, in and on top of which a great fire was to be made about dusk, so as to get the hole thoroughly heated and full of red-hot coals by the time tattoo sounded. Into this hole the camp-kettle was then set, with several pounds of fat pork on top of the beans, and securely covered with an inverted mess-pan. It was sunk into the red hot coals, by which it was completely concealed, and was left there all night to bake, one of the camp-guards throwing a log on the fire from time to time to keep matters going.

Early the next morning some one shook me roughly as I lay sleeping soundly in my tent: "Get up, Billy! breakfast is ready. Come to our tent. If you never ate baked beans before, you never ate anything worth eating." I found three or four of the boys seated around the camp-kettle, each with a tin plate on his knee and a spoon in his hand, doing their very best to establish the truth of the old adage, "The proof of the pudding is in the eating." Now, it is a far more difficult matter to describe the experience of the palate than of either the eye or the ear, and therefore I shall not attempt to tell how very good baked beans are.

The only trouble with a camp-kettle full of the delicious food was that it was gone too soon. Where did it get to, anyhow? It was something like Mike Dalton's quart of drink,—an irrational quantity, because it was too much for one and too little for two.

Still, too much of a good thing is too much, and one might get quite too much of beans (except in the state above described); however, I resolved, then and there, that if I should be fortunate enough to return home with good health, I would, if I ever had any, teach my children to sing the refrain to the tune sometimes called "Aunt Rhody," and to pull up sharp on the last word,—

"Beans for breakfast,
Beans for dinner,
Beans for supper,
Beans, *beans*, BEANS!"

July 17: Very hot. There was considerable dissatisfaction among the band boys. They thought that Colonel Bishop was not treating them exactly right by compelling them to do police duty. They said that the time occupied in cleaning up the camp ought to be put in by practising, and there was some talk of them returning to their companies. The colonel in return said that the entire regiment was on picket and guard duty every day, and the men must have rest; therefore the band, having no guard duty to do and no dress parades, should at least help out by doing police duty every afternoon to relieve the men who had been on duty all night. We concluded not to go back to our companies.

July 18 to 23: We remained in camp doing police duty, but no rehearsing. We heard that General McPherson had been killed in front of Atlanta.

Sunday, July 24: Attended church in a body in the morning. Dress parade in the evening. On the 25th, at 11 A.M., the regiment went to Chattanooga as guard to eleven hundred prisoners. 26th and 27th: Very quiet in camp, as the regiment was still absent. We heard the distant boom of cannon at Atlanta all day, which reminded us that there must be considerable activity in front. We knew that with Sherman in command the army was not liable to fall asleep or lie inactive.

July 28: Regiment returned from Chattanooga. Band serenaded General Joe Hooker.

He departed for Washington the next day under orders to report to the commander-in-chief. We remained in Marietta until August 19, and enjoyed ourselves as we did not expect to again.

Considering that the troops in the front had been under fire every day, while we were comparatively out of all danger, we had made some considerable improvement among our drafted men in drilling and the manual of arms. The regiment was in splendid condition, and were prepared to undertake and make a vigorous campaign against the enemy. On the 19th we marched twelve miles to the Chattahoochee River and encamped.

August 20: Marched fourteen miles in front of Atlanta and joined the brigade in the breastworks. The rebel breastworks were about one hundred yards distant, and the men were in plain sight.

Sunday, August 21: Warm and pleasant. We remained in camp with everything quiet along the line. During the day we heard the distant boom of artillery on our extreme left wing. We had lain in the trenches in front of Atlanta, under fire every day, from the 22d to the 25th, when we got orders to march at twelve o'clock midnight.

August 26: We broke camp at the hour named,

under orders to march as quietly as possible, and not to make any unnecessary noise. The officers sent all of their extra baggage to the rear. 27th: Weather very hot. We marched seven miles and countermarched, then halted and built breastworks. The enemy was following us. We lay in the edge of a piece of timber. We could distinctly see their wagons, and dense clouds of dust rose over the woods as the rebel troops marched southward.

Sunday, August 28: We marched at 5.30 A.M. southward in the direction of the Macon and Atlanta Railroad and encamped six miles north of it.

August 29: The Second Division of our corps destroyed a portion of the Montgomery and Atlanta Railroad. 30th: Very hot. We marched eleven miles. We were now south of Atlanta, and expected an engagement every day. Things were looking as though Sherman was getting the enemy cornered. 31st: Weather very hot. We marched to the front and drove the Confederates over the railroad. Heavy cannonading on our right.

September 1: Weather very hot. About 4 P.M. General Davis assaulted the enemy's lines in our front, sweeping all before him and capturing the greater part of Goven's brigade, including its commander. The troops on our right had been heavily engaged; and thus ended the battle of Jonesboro'.

At 2 A.M. on the morning of September 2 the sound of heavy cannonading was heard from the direction of Atlanta, twenty miles distant, indicating the evacuation of that place by General Hood. Without regarding these tokens, Sherman pressed on the next morning in pursuit of Hardee, but found it impossible to intercept his retreat.

We heard that the Twentieth Corps (Slocum's) had entered Atlanta and was in possession. Our corps remained and buried the dead and took care of the wounded.

September 3: Weather fine until midnight, when it commenced to rain and continued through the night and during the next day. We could still hear the boom of artillery in front. We remained here until the 7th, when we marched nine miles in the direction of Atlanta and encamped in a large cotton-field.

September 8: We marched nine miles, within two miles of Atlanta. We found that the rebels had this place very heavily fortified. 9th: Weather fine. Went to town on a pass. The destruction in the city was terrible. Our shells played havoc in the principal part of the city, and it was riddled up fearfully 10th: Weather hot. Remained in camp all day. We heard the joyful tidings of the death of John Morgan, the rebel guerilla. From September 11 to October 3 we remained in this camp and had battalion and regimental drill every day

On the 15th of September, R. G. Rhoades started for Cincinnati, to purchase a new set of band instruments. He had a twenty-days' furlough. We heard all sorts of rumors,—that Hood was in our rear marching into Nashville, and again that he was marching on to Louisville; and each one created more or less excitement, until the next was reported.

October 1: Colonel Bishop left us for Minnesota with a requisition from General Thomas for men to fill up the regiment, leaving Lieutenant-Colonel Uline in command.

On October 3 we broke camp and marched eight miles towards the Chattahoochee River, and lay over in the woods all night, the rain pouring down in torrents.

October 4: At daybreak, wet and hungry, we resumed our march. We accomplished ten miles and crossed the Chattahoochee River. There were a great many stragglers, the men having had no rest at night; and the intense heat caused them to become weary and tired.

October 5: Weather overcast and cloudy Marched fifteen miles, to Kenesaw Mountain, and went into camp at 9 P.M. It rained all night.

October 6: Rainy and disagreeable all forenoon, but in the afternoon it turned out clear and warm. Marched six miles. We had had no meat for four days, and the usual amount of grumbling was heard on all sides.

October 7: Weather pleasant. Our division was ordered to reconnoitre north of Lost Mountain. K Company skirmished with the Johnnies a short time during the day. We marched fifteen miles.

October 8: Cold and windy. Lay in camp until 4 P.M., then marched towards Ackworth, eight miles. We here got our first news of the battle of Altoona.

October 9: We remained in camp all day Weather very cold. We tried to ruminate in our minds what the matter was. Last month we were fighting facing south; now we had the rebel army between us and Nashville, and again faced back north. We could not conceive what was the matter with Sherman?

October 10: Remained in camp until 4 P.M., then broke camp and marched all night, passing over the battle-field of Altoona Heights. Here we found the Fourth Minnesota Regiment, who took a conspicuous part in the fight. We stopped for a short time and drank a cup of coffee, which the boys of the Fourth made for us, for which we returned our heart-felt thanks. We resumed our march until daylight, having marched fifteen miles.

October 11: Weather fine. We marched thirteen miles to Kingston, Ga., and went into camp.

October 13: Very hot. Remained in camp during the heat of the day, and at 7 P.M. broke camp and were on the road all night, making only ten miles.

October 14: Weather cool. We marched twenty miles to Resaca and encamped on the Etowah River.

October 15: Weather pleasant. We marched eight miles, climbed the Rocky-Faced Mountain, and encamped on top. 16th: Weather very pleasant. We marched down the north side of the mountain, through Snake Creek Gap, and encamped near Taylor's Ridge. 17th: Lay in camp all day, and sent back extra baggage. 18th: Weather pleasant. Marched sixteen miles, passing over Taylor's Ridge. 19th: Weather pleasant. We crossed the Chattanooga River. Marched eight miles. 20th: Weather pleasant. Passed through Somerville and encamped near Gailsville, Ga., on the Coosa River. 21st: Weather pleasant. Remained in camp until 3 P.M., after which our brigade was ordered to Gailsville for duty. 22d: Very cool all day Men were detailed to run the grist-mill, to grind corn for meal; and others to repair the bridge over the Coosa River.

Sunday, October 23: Weather pleasant. Remained in camp, repairing our clothing and doing some washing.

October 24: Weather warm and pleasant. I went out foraging and had quite a little adventure. About ten o'clock I found myself about six miles from camp, on the Coosa River, and, seeing some citrons in a field close to the river bank, I went to look at them. I was examining one of them when I heard the reports of two guns and the zip, zip of the bullets close to me. On looking over the river I saw two rebel cavalrymen near a corn-fodder stack, and it took me but a moment to make myself scarce in that locality. About sixty yards distant was a deep ravine, which was covered with a canebrake. Towards this I made my way in double-quick time. In the mean time they fired two more shots, which whistled in close proximity. After reaching the cover of the ravine I followed it up to the head and came out in a farm-yard, where I found four boys of the Eighty-third Illinois. To them I related my adventure, and they proposed to go back and stir the rebs up a little. I went back the route I had taken in my retreat, and as we reached the brow of the ravine, we saw that two more men had joined the former two that fired at me.

My comrades had repeating rifles, and they immediately opened up on them; but, being so excited, they fired wild. We had the satisfaction, however, of seeing them mount their horses and gallop away, while my friends continued to grind out shot after shot at them, while I, unarmed, was a quiet spectator of the fusilade. The Johnnies showed some very fine generalship in their retreat. While our boys were firing at them they kept the fodder-stack between themselves and us, which saved them from being killed.

October 25: Weather fine. A large foraging party was sent out, and returned late in the evening with plenty of pork, beef, and corn-meal. 26th and 27th: It rained most of the time, which kept the boys in their little shelter-tents.

Immediately in front of our camp was the head-quarters of General Sherman, whom we saw at all hours of the day and night, marching back and forth in front of his tent, with his head bowed, chin on his breast, and his arms locked behind him. That night he made the rounds all night with the guard in front of his tent, occasionally stopping in front of the fire to talk a moment with him, then resuming his steady march. I had no doubt but that he was planning some campaign that would surprise the natives.

October 28: Weather clear and cool. As

expected, we received orders to march the next day at 4 A.M.

October 29 : Weather pleasant. We moved at the appointed time, and marched south all day Made twenty miles and encamped.

October 30: Weather cool. We marched six miles to Rome, Ga., and encamped on the Oostenaula River. I received my new drum from Cincinnati, and was much pleased with it, and determined to make it lively for the boys.

October 31 : Warm and pleasant. We were mustered for pay. Received a large mail for the regiment.

November 1: Pleasant and warm. We had orders to wash up all blankets and clothing. In the afternoon we received two months' pay.

November 2 : Cold rain all day. We marched thirteen miles to Kingston, Ga., where we expected to find Rhoades, and were much disappointed in finding that he had not arrived. 3d : Raining all day Rhoades, our band-master, arrived with the new instruments. 4th : Raw, cold wind. The boys tried their new instruments and were highly pleased with them. 5th : Cold and cloudy. Ripley and Mart. Smith arrived from Chattanooga. 6th : Rainy and disagreeable. Lay in the tents all day. 7th : We made our first appearance with our new silver instruments and created quite a furor.

November 8: This was election-day for President, the proudest day of my life. I was eighteen years and four months old, and cast my first ballot, which was for Abraham Lincoln. Our company cast thirty-five ballots, all for Lincoln. The McClellan men were scarce in our regiment.

November 9: Cool and disagreeable. On the 11th, Colonel Bishop rejoined us with eighty-eight recruits, which were immediately distributed to the several companies. 12th: Weather pleasant. Marched sixteen miles.

Sunday, November 13: Marched eighteen miles and tore up three miles of the Atlanta and Chattanooga Railroad. 14th: Marched twenty-five miles from Big Shanty to Chattahoochee River.

November 15: Weather cloudy, but warm and pleasant. Marched nine miles to Atlanta, and at night we destroyed the city by fire. A grand and awful spectacle it presented to the beholder. By order, the chief engineer had destroyed by powder and fire all the storehouses, depot-buildings, and machine-shops. The heaven was one expanse of lurid fire; the air was filled with flying burning cinders. Buildings, covering two hundred acres were in ruins or in flames; every instant there was the sharp detonation of the smothered, booming sound of exploding shells and powder concealed in the buildings, and then the sparks and flames would shoot up into the black and red roof, scattering cinders far and wide.

These were the machine-shops where had been forged and cast the rebel cannon, shot, and shells that had carried death to many a brave defender of our nation's honor.

The warehouses had been the receptacles of munitions of war, stored there to be used for our destruction.

This city, next to Richmond, furnished more material for prosecuting the war than any other in the South.

A brigade of Massachusetts soldiers were the only troops then left in the town; they were the last to leave it. That night I heard the really fine band of the Thirty-third Massachusetts playing "John Brown's soul goes marching on" by the light of the burning building. I never heard that noble anthem when it was so grand, so solemn, and so inspiring.

November 16: Warm and pleasant. We marched sixteen miles towards Augusta, Ga., through a country that seemed to have raised nothing but cotton. It looked worn out; the fences were down and the buildings in a more or less dilapidated condition. 17th: Hot. We marched eighteen miles. Destroyed a large section of the Atlanta and Augusta Railroad. Passed through a much finer country than on the previous day

November 18: Warm. Our division tore up several miles of railroad. Passed through the village of Covington, Ga. 19th: Rainy and cloudy all day Marched twelve miles. 20th: Weather fine. Marched through some very beautiful country, leaving fifteen miles behind us. 21st: Marched steadily all day until 10 P.M., covering twenty miles. Weather warm and pleasant. The army foraged on the country during our march. To this end each brigade commander organized a good and sufficient foraging party,—we called them "Bummers,"—under the command of one or more discreet officers, who gathered near the route travelled corn or forage of any kind, meat of all kinds, vegetables, corn-meal, or whatever was needed by the command. Preserves and sweet-meats were also not refused. Their aim was at all times to keep in the wagon-trains at least ten days' rations for the command and three days' forage. Soldiers were ordered not to enter the dwellings of the inhabitants or commit any trespass. During a halt or while in camp we were permitted to gather turnips, sweet-potatoes, yams, and other vegetables, and drive in to our camps all stock we found. To the regular foraging parties was intrusted the gathering of provisions and forage at any distance from the road travelled.

November 21: Marched twenty miles, encamping at midnight. 22d: Warm and pleasant. Marched fifteen miles. 23d: Marched ten miles to Milledgeville, the capital of Georgia. A few days before our arrival at Milledgeville the State Legislature, then assembled at the capitol, had hurriedly absconded on hearing of Sherman's approach. The panic seemed to have spread to the citizens, and the trains out of Milledgeville were crowded to overflowing; and at the most extravagant prices. Private vehicles were pressed into service by the fugitives. Only a few of us entered the city. The magazines, arsenals, depots, factories, and storehouses containing property belonging to the Confederate government were burned; also some seventeen hundred bales of cotton. Private dwellings were respected, and no instance occurred of pillage or of insult to the people. General Sherman occupied the executive mansion of Governor Brown, who had not waited to receive the compliments of his distinguished visitor, but had removed his furniture, taking good care, the darkies say, to ship even his cabbage.

November 24: The army moved over the Oconee River. Our division remained as rear guard. Weather warm during the day, but the nights were very cold.

November 25: Left the city at 9 A.M. Burnt the bridge over the river at this place. Marched sixteen miles, crossing the Oconee River. We lost poor Simmers, the drummer of Company G, during the night. The poor fellow, being unable to keep up, lay down somewhere along the road, and was captured by the cavalry that were following us up. I took his blanket and drum to relieve him, but he was too fatigued to follow, saying to me, "Oh, let me rest; let me sleep a short time, then I will follow on." I tried to keep him under my eye all the time, but he finally eluded me, and when we again stopped for a short rest he was not to be found, and by that time was most likely a prisoner. I pitied the poor fellow. I was afraid he would never live to return home.

November 26: Warm and pleasant. Marched sixteen miles, passing through Sandersville. 27th: During the day it was very warm, but the nights were very cold. We crossed the Ogeechee River, having marched sixteen miles. 28th: Weather pleasant. We marched six miles, recrossing the Ogeechee, and destroyed the small village of Louisville, Ga. 29th: Weather warm and pleasant. Remained in camp all day. 30th: Very hot. Heavy firing in front. We moved camp a short distance to the front.

December 1: Skirmished with the rebs all day, driving them six miles. 2d: Weather very hot. We marched twelve miles, skirmishing most of the day. 3d: Marched eight miles, being compelled to skirmish every foot we gained. Destroyed some railroad. Sunday, December 4: We acted as support to General Kilpatrick's division of cavalry, who drove the enemy through Swainsboro'. Marched twenty miles. 5th: After having marched eastward for two days, we turned and marched due south eighteen miles through a poor sandy country. 6th: Marched fifteen miles through heavy, dense forests, some trees towering up to a height of a hundred feet. 7th: Disagreeable and cold rain all day. Marched fourteen miles. 8th: Hot. Marched twenty miles. 9th: Warm and pleasant. Marched eight miles. Did considerable skirmishing. One man in K Company was wounded. 10th: Pleasant. We marched six miles, destroying some of the Charleston and Savannah Railroad.

Sunday, December 10: We marched but two miles, stopping to tear up a small section of railroad. We also attempted to destroy a trestlework that led over the rice-fields to the Savannah River, but a rebel gunboat made it too unpleasant for us, so we had to give up that job. Here is where we first saw the process of threshing, hulling, and cleaning rice, a mill being close to where we were at work.

Colonel Bishop gave orders that the men should not leave or go one hundred yards from the stacks, as it was expected that the woods in the near vicinity was a cover for the rebel cavalry, who had been following us, gobbling up our stragglers who had wandered too far away from the main body.

Not thinking that this order included me, and not having to work on the railroad track, I thought I would go out on a little foraging expedition of my own while the regiment was destroying the railroad.

I went about a mile and a half, and came to a very fine plantation, where the white folks had all run off, leaving nobody at home but an old negro couple, and I was the first Union soldier they had seen. After I told them that they were now free and could go where they wished, and that I was one of "Massa Lincum's" soldiers, their joy knew no bounds. Nothing was too good for me; but knowing that my time was necessarily short, I told them I wanted something to eat. The old darky proceeded to the garden and dug about a peck of yams, and the old lady went to the barn and got me about two dozen eggs. She also gave me a piece of bacon. I thanked them kindly and started back to the camp. In passing by the barn, I noticed two nice fat cows, and said to myself, "If Sam Bowler only had them to kill for the regiment!" Sam was our commissary

In a short time I arrived in sight of the regiment, and carefully looked up and down the line to see that the colonel was nowhere near. Not seeing him, I marched up to about where our left flank would be and tried to get around on the other side of the track where the band boys were; but what was my surprise when I ran right onto the colonel, sitting down behind a pile of railroad-ties. I came up to within ten feet of him.

He looked at me and saw that I had a rubber blanket over my shoulder with something in it, and asked, "What have you got in your blanket?" I answered, "Potatoes." "What have you got in your handkerchief?" "Eggs," I replied. "Where did you get them?" he again asked. "Oh," said I, "about two hundred yards from here." "Is that so?" said he. "That's so," said I. "About two hundred yards from here?" he remarked. I answered with a nice little "Yes, sir," and commenced to tell him about the two nice fat cows that I had seen, hoping he would forget about the potatoes and eggs, but he didn't forget worth a cent.

He told me he would talk "cows" a little later, and ordered me to put my potatoes and eggs on the ground, and go down on the railroad and go to work tearing up the track. I never got humpbacked from the amount of work I did. I principally kept one eye on the colonel and the other on the potatoes and eggs.

It was not long before the colonel's cook (Place, I think his name was) came along and gathered up the aforesaid articles. I knew the colonel did not know anything about it; of course not. Colonels don't eat eggs. I did considerable talking to Place about it; but he took them all the same, saying, "I can't see potatoes and eggs lying around loose, when I know the colonel is just suffering with hunger." Well, that was the last I saw of the eggs and yams.

We encamped close by for the night, and it commenced to rain, with thunder and lightning.

Anybody who has been in the South knows that it is dark at such times. I had just got nicely curled up in my blanket, in my sheltertent, when the colonel's orderly came to me and said, "The colonel wants to see you." Throwing my poncho over my head, I proceeded to the colonel's tent, thinking, probably, he had some difficult military problem he wanted me to solve. But consternation was depicted on my countenance when he asked me if I had not told him during the day that I knew where there were two nice fat cows. I drawled out a mighty long "Yes, sir," after which he said, "You will now report to Lieutenant McCoy, who is officer of the day, and he will take two men besides yourself and bring those cows into camp, and turn them over to Bowler, and tell him to have them killed and issued to the men in the morning, after which you will report to me again."

I bid the colonel good-night, and, in the darkness and rain, hunted up the guard-tent. I found Lieutenant McCoy, gave him my orders, and got a good damning from him for telling the colonel about the cows. We finally got started, and I, as the guide, directed them through the dense pine forest the best I knew how, having been over the road but once before myself. Fortunately, I found the plantation all right, also the cows, but we had no ropes. Now here was a quandary We had no lantern, and how were we to lead the cows back to camp? In feeling around in the dark, I found an old harness and took the lines out of it, and with these we led them back to camp, but before we got there a sad calamity befell me.

Surrounding the plantation was a wide and deep ditch, over which a bridge was made to raise and lower whenever in use. In going over this, the cow I was leading, being wild, started and ran diagonally across the bridge, and it being so dark that it was impossible to see your hand before you, every vivid flash of lightning would so blind us that for a few moments we were, as it seemed, in inky darkness.

As the cow ran she dragged me along; but I hung on to her like grim death, and ran off the bridge, falling into the ditch, down at least eight feet. I clung to the bank or side of the ditch the best I could, it being soft and slimy from the rain, until my comrades helped me out. The leather strap with which the cow was tied was wet and slippery, and, of course, I could not hold her. The other cow was held by one of the other boys, who was fortunate enough not to fall off the bridge. She continued to bellow, which kept the one which got loose from getting far away from us. In a short time we had caught her again, and succeeded in arriving in camp without any further mishap.

I then proceeded to notify Sam Bowler, who by this time was sleeping soundly in his tent. After waking him up and giving him the colonel's orders, I received another cursing and damning for telling the colonel about the cows. I waited to see that Sam got up, and then turned our stock over to him. Afterwards, according to orders, I reported to Colonel Bishop, and informed him that we had returned with the cows.

The colonel being in bed, rose to a sitting posture and remarked, "Hereafter, when I give the regiment an order, I want you to understand that it includes you as well as any other member of the regiment; and sending you after the cows you may consider a punishment for your offence." He bid me good-night, and then said, "Go and tell Bowler to give you a piece of the liver."

I thought at the time that the eggs and yams didn't set well on his stomach, or that they had a bad effect on his liver. "All right, colonel."

When I gave Bowler the colonel's order about the liver, he said, "Young fellow, you just skip to your tent. The cows *h*ain't got no liver. These *h*are Confederate cows. Nothing but good Union cows 'ave liver. So, now, you skip. You got no business to tell the colonel about those cows, *h*and get me *h*out *h*ov my good warm bed to kill 'em." I saw that my worthy English friend was in no mood to talk any more.

Before retiring I took off all my wet clothes and put on some dry ones, and soon forgot my troubles in a sound and refreshing sleep, only to be awakened on the morning of the 12th by the distant boom of artillery in the direction of the coast, which continued off and on all day.

The 13th was warm and pleasant. We marched southwest seven miles, and heard heavy firing in the direction of Savannah.

14th: Pleasant and warm. Remained in camp all day We were very short of rations.

December 15: Moved camp about half a mile towards Savannah. We are now living on plain rice, without salt. We first chopped a trough-like hole in a log, then laid the heads of the rice-sheaves in it, and with a club threshed the grains out; then we rubbed the kernels between our hands to clear it of hulls; after which we used our lungs for a fanning mill, placing the rice, hulls, sand, and all, in a tin plate and blowing until we had it free from hulls; but the sand still remained, and, like the rice, sunk to the bottom and could not be cleaned out; so we had to cook the rice with the sand in it.

In eating it we dared not chew it, but swallowed it whole. By doing so we did not feel the grit until we got through, then, after rinsing the mouth, we soon forgot that we had been filling up on sand mixed with a little rice.

December 16: Warm and pleasant. The brigade went out foraging for a three-days' trip. The band remained in camp. 11th to 18th: Quiet in camp. Regiment still absent. 19th: Still comfortably warm. The regiment returned at 4 P.M. very much fatigued. They brought their wagons back all well loaded with forage. 20th: Warm and pleasant. Remained in camp. Nothing transpired worthy of note.

December 21: Warm. Hardee evacuated Savannah, leaving all of his artillery, amounting to one hundred and twenty pieces, and seventeen hundred bales of cotton.

December 22: Weather cold, with a strong, cutting wind from the coast. We marched six miles to within one mile of Savannah and went into camp.

December 23: Weather clear and cold. Went and took a view of the city, and was surprised to see such a beautiful place. The streets were all very wide, particularly Bull Street, which had a beautiful little park at the crossing of every street. It had three walks the full length of the street,—one down through the middle, that passed through the parks, and one on each side. Live-oak-trees shaded the entire street and parks. I noticed in one of the parks a beautiful statue erected to the memory of Count Pulaski, who fell mortally wounded at the siege of this place, October 9, 1779. The residence portion of the city had some very fine and tasty buildings. The churches and public buildings were also of very fine architecture. Everything in the city indicated wealth and refinement.

December 24: Rather warmer. As rations were yet very scarce, we were informed that a short distance below Savannah were several large oyster-beds. A detail of men and two teams went down to see if it was possible to procure enough for a Christmas dinner for the regiment.

On their return we found they had succeeded in filling one wagon-box; but they were of a very inferior quality. The natives called them the "cluster oyster." There were two to five in one bunch, and hard to get out. So our Christmas dinner did not consist of turkey with oyster filling and cranberry sauce.

What a glorious camp-fire we had that Christmas eve of 1864! It makes me rub my hands together to think of it. The nights were getting cold and frosty, so that it was impossible to sleep under our little shelter-tents with comfort; and so, half the night was spent around the blazing fires in front of our tents.

I always took care that there should be a blazing good fire for our little squad, anyhow. My duties were light and left me time, which I found I could spend with pleasure in swinging an axe. Hickory and white-oak saplings were my favorites, and I had them piled up as high as my head on wooden fire-dogs. What a glorious crackle we had by midnight!

We could go out to the fire at any time of night we pleased (and we were pretty sure to go out three or four times a night, for it was too cold to sleep in the tent more than an hour at a stretch), and we would always find half a dozen

CHRISTMAS EVE AROUND THE CAMP-FIRE AT SAVANNAH.

of the boys sitting about the fire-logs, smoking their pipes, telling yarns, or singing snatches of old songs.

Rhoades, Ripley, Chase, and Chamberlain were all good singers. I hoped that we might live to recall those weird night-scenes of army-life,— the blazing fires, the groups of swarthy men that gathered about them in the darkness of the forests, where the lights and shadows danced and played all night long, and the rows of little white tents covered with frost. It looked quite poetical in the retrospect, but I fear it was sometimes prosy enough in the reality

"If you fellows would stop your everlasting arguing there, and go out and bring in some wood, it would be a good deal better; for if we don't have a big camp-fire to-night we'll freeze in this snow-storm."

So saying, Kelsey Chase threw down the butt-end of a pine-sapling, which he had been half-dragging, half-carrying out of the woods in which we were encamped, and, axe in hand, fell to work with a will.

There was, indeed, some need to follow Kelsey's advice, for it was snowing fast and was getting bitterly cold, the wind coming straight off the coast, which was but a few miles south of the camp.

It was Christmas eve, and here we were with

no protection but our little shelter-tents pitched on the hard, frozen ground. It was hard to be homeless at this merry season of the year, when folks up North were having such happy times, wasn't it? But it was wonderful how elastic the spirits of our soldiers were, and how jolly they could be under the most adverse circumstances.

Chamberlain spoke: "Well, Chase, you hadn't any business to put me out of the mess. That was a mean trick, any way you take it."

"If we hadn't put you out of our mess, you'd have eaten up all the rations that were issued to the three of us. You are an awful glutton," chimed in Brunner.

"Say, boys! I move we organize ourselves into a court and try this case," said Billy Sibley. "They've been arguing and arguing about this thing the whole day, and it's time to take it up and put an end to it. The case is,—let's see,—what'll we call it? I'm not very good at this legal lingo; but I suppose if we call it a 'motion to quash a writ of ejectment,' or something of that sort, we'll be within the lines of the law. Let me now state the case: Chamberlain *versus* Brunner and Chase. These three, all members of the Second Minnesota, after having lived, messed, and sojourned together peaceably for a year or more, have had of late some disagreement, quarrel, squabble, fracas, or general tearing-out. The result of which said disagreement, quarrel, squabble, etc., etc., has been that the hereinbefore Chamberlain has been thrown out of the mess and left to the cold charities of the camp; and he, the said Chamberlain, now lodges a due and formal complaint before this honorable court, presently sitting on this pile of pine brush, and humbly prays and petitions reinstatement in his just rights and claims, *sine qua non, e pluribus unum, pro bono publico!* Silence in the court!"

To organize ourselves into a court of justice was a matter of a few moments. Vandyke was declared the judge, Wesley Stewart and Mart Smith associates. A jury of six men, good and true, was speedily empanelled. Attorneys, sheriff, and clerk were appointed, and in less time than it takes to narrate it we were seated on piles of pine brush, around a roaring campfire, with snow falling fast, trying the celebrated case of "Chamberlain *versus* Brunner and Chase." And a world of merriment we had out of it, you may well believe.

When the jury, after having retired for a few moments behind a pine-tree, brought in a verdict for the plaintiff, it was full one o'clock on Christmas morning, and we began to drop off to sleep, some rolling themselves up in their blankets and overcoats and lying down, Indian-fashion, feet to the fire, while others crept off to their cold shelter-tents under the snow-laden pine-trees for what poor rest they could find, jocularly wishing each other a "Merry Christmas!"

December 25: Cold and windy Snow still on the ground; but in the afternoon it warmed up and commenced to melt, and by night the ground was entirely clear of snow, leaving the ground very muddy. The camp was very quiet. The boys were standing in groups around the fire and discussing the menu of the Christmas dinner.

December 26: Cool and cloudy Received orders to prepare for grand review the next day; otherwise nothing new occurred. 27th: Weather warm and pleasant. We marched to the city and passed in review before General W T. Sherman. Regiment returned to camp at 2.30 P.M., and immediately went on picket. 28th: Cold and rainy and very disagreeable. We were compelled to remain in our shelter-tents all day. 29th: Warm and pleasant. Rumor in camp that General Lee had surrendered to General Grant.

December 30: Pleasant. The boys were engaged in building little log huts, and were putting in fireplaces and making improvements, as if they were going to put in the remainder of their term of service here.

December 31: Weather cold and windy. Remained in camp and tried to make ourselves as comfortable as possible. Since January 1, 1864, we had travelled two thousand six hundred and eighty-nine miles.

January 1, 1865: Cold, cloudy, and dreary. A long, lank, lean Georgian came into camp, and espied Bob Bailey, our hospital steward, who was rather a diminutive fellow, weighing about ninety or a hundred pounds. After looking him all over, he finally approached him, remarking,—

"What did they bring you down here for?"

"Oh!" replied Bob, "to kill all the Confederates I should come across."

"They did? Well, did you ever kill anybody?"

"Oh, yes," said Bob, "lots of 'em,—lots of 'em, sir."

"You don't tell me!" said the Georgian; "and, if I might be pert enough to ask, how do you generally kill them?"

"Well," replied Bob, "I never like to tell, because bragging is not in my line; but I will tell you. You see, I never liked this thing of shooting people. It seemed to me a barbarous business; and, besides, I was a kind of Quaker, and had conscientious scruples about bearing arms. And so, when the war broke out and I found I'd have to enter the army, maybe, whether I wanted to or not, I enlisted and got in as pill dispenser, thinking in that position I wouldn't have to kill anybody with a gun, but with blue mass I couldn't help it. But I found that even a hospital steward had to take a hand at killing people; and the principal way I took for it was this: I always managed to have a good swift horse, and as soon as things would begin to look like fighting and the big guns would begin to boom, why, I'd clap spurs to my horse and make for the rear as fast as ever I could. And then when your people would come after me, they never could catch me; they'd always get out of breath trying to keep up to me; and in that way I've killed hundreds and hundreds of your people, sir,—thousands of them,—and all without powder or ball. They couldn't catch me, and always died for the want of breath trying to get hold of me."

"Well," the Georgian remarked, "for a small man, you are the biggest liar I ever saw."

January 2: Warm and pleasant. Moved camp half a mile nearer the city. Cleared off the rubbish and wood from the camp-ground preparatory to establishing a new camp.

January 3: The whole regiment were busily engaged chopping logs and poles with which to erect their little huts. I sprained my back, and was unable to move. The surgeon gave me some liniment, but it did no good.

From January 4 to the 15th we remained at this camp, drilling and doing camp and police duty. Every other day we visited the city. One evening as a few of the boys were returning from the theatre, I being among them, we passed a fine residence, where there were some ladies in the second-story window, singing the "Bonny Blue Flag" and "Maryland, My Maryland." We stopped and listened a few moments, and when they got through, we commenced and sung that grand old anthem, the "Star-Spangled Banner."

I don't think there ever was such a surprise in that house before. I don't think the "Star-Spangled Banner" ever sounded grander or sweeter than it did that night in the still, dark streets of Savannah, sung by the boys in blue. They raised the window and requested us to sing the "Red, White, and Blue," and the ladies accompanied us. They thanked us, bid us goodnight, and invited us to come down some evening and repeat the programme.

January 15: Moved camp to the Grand Central Depot. The regiment was quartered in the main building, and the head-quarters and band occupied the offices. We had very comfortable quarters. We remained here doing provost duty until January 19, when we were relieved by the Nineteenth New Hampshire Regiment.

January 20: We marched eight miles and joined the brigade. Our bugler, Sandine, had been on a toot for some time and was left behind. Colonel Bishop had made several inquiries in regard to his absence. The colonel knew his failings, and a reprimand when he returned would be the extent of his punishment. We lay here until the 25th, and it rained during most of the time. The rivers were very high and the low lands all more or less flooded, and if the soil were anything but sand it would be impossible to move the army, as the roads would be impassable. We marched that day nine miles to Springfield and encamped.

January 27: Warm and cloudy We marched two miles on the Sister's Ferry Road. 28th: Warm and pleasant. We marched ten miles north to Millan and Savannah Railroad and encamped.

January 29: Sandine succeeded in reaching the regiment, and gave the colonel as an excuse for his absence that he had followed some troops that were crossing the Savannah River on pontoons at Savannah, and, after marching with them one day, he found that it was part of some other corps. He then retraced his steps to Savannah, where he found that his regiment had gone north on the Sister's Ferry Road. After a week's absence he was considerably disfigured, but still able to bring out the clarion notes from his bugle, and was all right again after the "commissary" had worked out of him.

January 30: Weather warm and pleasant. The foragers returned to camp with forty-seven head of fine cattle.

January 31: Everything quiet in camp. The pontoniers were laying pontoons across the river; the water being so high, they had considerable difficulty in completing the bridge.

February 1 to 5: Remained here, waiting for the completion of the pontoons. On the 3d, General Kilpatrick crossed over into South Carolina with his division of cavalry, and as he went onto the bridge he remarked to one of the officers standing near, "There will be d—n little left for you boys to destroy after I have passed through that hell-hole of secession," pointing to the opposite shore.

On February 5 we marched with unfurled flags, men cheering, and singing "Tramp, tramp," etc., crossing the Savannah River into South Carolina. Our army did not lack enthusiasm, and the prospect of a march through South Carolina was one that was exceedingly relished.

The general feeling of the North towards

Charleston may be inferred from General Halleck's suggestion to Sherman,—" Should you capture Charleston, I hope that by accident the place may be destroyed; and if a little salt be sown on its site, it may prevent the growth of future crops of nullification and secession."

Poor South Carolina! She was sandwiched in between two States who looked upon her as the original source of their past madness and their present trouble.

February 6: We were building corduroy roads for the teams to follow us, and we made but slow progress. We encamped at night in a burr-oak grove. The soil so far had been very sandy. 7th: Rainy and cloudy. We marched nine miles, passing through Robinsonville to the Augusta Turnpike.

Wednesday, February 8: Warm and very windy. We marched eleven miles. The whole army was burning with the insatiable desire to wreak vengeance on South Carolina. I almost trembled at her fate, but felt that she deserved all that seemed in store for her.

February 9: Warm and pleasant. Marched twenty miles and destroyed all the houses, barns, and fences on our route.

February 10: Marched twenty-five miles to Barnwell Court-House, the county seat, where we found that General Kilpatrick, who was in advance of us, had destroyed the greater part of the city.

February 11: We marched at 6 A.M., and the small portion of the town that Kilpatrick left intact was destroyed by our division. We marched twelve miles. The weather was warm and pleasant. Bright sunshine overhead all day.

February 12: Marched twelve miles. Destroyed six miles of the Augusta and Charleston Railroad, and encamped at 9 P.M. 13th: We marched eight miles to the South Edisto River and encamped. The men were all more or less worn out. We had some pretty heavy marching that week. 14th: Rained all day. Marched sixteen miles. Crossed the South and North Edisto Rivers. Encamped on the north bank of the North Edisto. 15th: Our brigade was detailed for rear guard, and we were required to repair the roads as we advanced. The wagons were stuck all along the roads for miles. Marched but ten miles. 16th: Marched sixteen miles. Passed through Lexington Court-House. The troops destroyed every house along the road.

February 17: Cold and cloudy We lay along the roads all day waiting for the troops ahead of us to cross the Saluda River, and at 7.30 P.M. we commenced to move. We crossed the Saluda, a very swift and muddy stream. The fences and buildings, the entire length of our day's march, were burning, and the smoke very nearly suffocated us. We marched that day but eight miles.

February 18: Worked on the roads all day, repairing them, so that the artillery and supply-trains could follow.

Sabbath, February 19: Not a cloud in the sky, and so warm and pleasant. This was truly God's day, and we were engaged in the hellish work of destroying and burning property. We crossed the Broad River and destroyed the village of Alston, the junction of the Columbia and Greenville and Columbia and Charleston Railroads. Here we found considerable rolling-stock, which we run out on a trestle-work, and when we marched away the trestle-work and cars were one mass of flames. We marched ten miles.

February 20: Passed through a fine farming country, with plenty of forage, plenty of meat and yams, and we lived on the top shelf.

February 21: Weather could not be better. We marched twenty miles through a beautiful country and encamped at night at Winnsboro' We were at noon in the section where General Francis Marion, of Revolutionary fame, a celebrated partisan officer, who warred against the

WRECKING THE RAILWAY ON THE MARCH TO THE SEA.

British and Tories in South Carolina and Georgia, feasted the British officer on roast potatoes. For a dish he utilized a piece of bark.

February 22: Marched twelve miles and destroyed four miles of the Columbia and Richmond Railroad. The weather was warm and pleasant, similar to our Minnesota May. 23d: Marched southeast on the Camden Road fifteen miles and encamped in the dense pine forests. 24th: Rained all day Lay in camp waiting for the pontoniers to lay a bridge over Wateree River. 25th: Ordered to cross the river. We marched to the river with the expectation of crossing, but the flood had broken the bridge, and portions of it had floated down the stream. We were compelled to remain here until it was again repaired. Weather rainy and cloudy 26th: Rained all day. We remained in camp until 7 P.M.; then, with pitch-pine knots burning for torches, we crossed the pontoons to the east bank.

February 27: Cloudy and misty. We marched ten miles and encamped. We marched usually four abreast, but made no effort to keep step; for marching in that way, though good enough for a mile or so, or on dress parade, would soon become intolerable if kept up for any length of time or any great distance.

In "rout steps" each man picked his way,

selecting his steps at his pleasure, and carrying or shifting his arms at his convenience. Even then, marching is no easy matter, especially when it is raining, and you are marching over a clay soil,—and it did seem to us that the soil about the Wateree River was the toughest and most slippery clay in the world, at least in the roads that wound, serpent-like, around the hills, among which we were marching, where, as we all knew, many a poor mule, during our march, had stuck fast and had to be literally pulled out or left to die in his tracks, after the harness had been ripped off his back.

February 28: Worked all day with the wagon-trains. They were stuck in the mud all along the road, for we made but eleven miles. We were very short of rations, and were living on what is called the "nigger-pea."

March 1: We marched twelve miles. The roads were filled with broken fence-rails for the entire length of our march, some lying lengthwise, others crosswise, and others with their ends sticking up from two to four feet. Through this we were compelled to march. The afternoon wore on, night set in, and we began to wonder, in all our simplicity, whether Sherman expected us to march all night as well as all day.

To make matters still worse, as night fell, dark and drizzling, we left the main road and came out on the high ground of those regions; and if we never before knew what South Carolina mud was like, we knew it then. It was not only knee-deep, but so sticky that when we set one foot down we could scarcely pull the other out.

We had a little darky along with us on this march who had an experience which was quite provoking to him, as it was amusing to us. The darky's name was Bill. Other name he had none, except "Shorty," which had been given him by the boys because of his remarkable short stature. Although he was strong as a man and quite as old featured, he was, nevertheless, so dwarfed in size that the name "Shorty" seemed to become him better than his original name.

Well, "Shorty" had been employed by one of the officers as cook, or, as seemed more likely on the present occasion, as a sort of pack-mule, for the officer, having an eye to comfort on the march, had loaded the poor darky with a pack of blankets, tent, pans, kettles, and general camp equipage, so large and bulky that it is no exaggeration to say that "Shorty's" pack was quite as large as himself. All along it had been a wonder to us how he had managed to pull through so far with all those big bundles on his back; but, with strength far beyond his size, he had trudged doggedly on in the rear of the regiment, over hill and through field, until we came at nightfall out on the main road again. Then, like many other pack-mules, he stuck fast in the mud, so that, puff and pull as he might, he could not pull either foot out, and had to be dragged out by two men, to the great merriment of all who in the growing darkness were aware of his misfortune.

At length it became so dark that no one was able to see an inch before his face. Torches were then lighted; then we forded a creek; and on and on we went, till at length we were allowed to halt and fall out on either side of the road into a last-year's corn-field to make fire and cook coffee.

To make a fire was a comparatively easy matter, notwithstanding the rain. Some one or other always had matches, and there were plenty of pitch-pine knots at hand, which were dry enough when split open with a hatchet or an axe. In a few moments the fence around the corn-field was carried off rail by rail, and everywhere was heard the sound of axes and hatchets, the premonitory symptoms of roaring camp-fires, which were soon everywhere blazing along the road.

March 2: Rained all day. We marched twenty miles. The roads were in a horrible condition, and we lay in the woods all night in our wet clothes, as it rained all night. We had but the clothes which were on our backs, and of course could not change, so matters were mighty uncomfortable until daylight of the 3d, which brought us no comfort. The rain continued all day With a cup of coffee and a few black peas for breakfast, we continued our march northward. We passed over twenty-one miles of South Carolina territory, and our camp at night was a repetition of the night before. We were cold, wet, and hungry.

March 4: Still rainy. The roads were very muddy and soft. There was at least twelve inches of mud underfoot. We marched fourteen miles and crossed over the line into North Carolina.

Sunday, March 5: Weather clear and warm; I hoped that the rainy season had passed. We marched eight miles to the Great Pedee River and encamped. We were sunburnt and covered with dirt, so that a swim in the river would be refreshing indeed.

Having learned from one of the officers that the intention evidently was to remain where we were until the entire corps should come up, and that we should probably cross the river at, or somewhere near, that point, we resolved to risk it. So, over a corn-field we started, at a good pace, Billy Wagner—or, by the way, "Jasper"—

and I. We had not gone far when we discovered a mule tied up, in a clump of bushes, with a rope. And this long-eared animal, as Gothic as Bonaparte in his style of architecture, we decided, after a solemn council of war, to declare contraband, and forthwith we impressed him into service, intending to return him, after our bath, on our return to camp. Untying the mule from the bush, we mounted, "Jasper" in front and I on behind, each armed with a switch, and we rode along gayly enough, with our feet dangling among the corn-stalks.

For a while all went well. We fell to talking about the direction we had come since leaving camp, and "Jasper," who was usually good authority on matters geographical and astronomical on the march (he was known in the company as "the compass"), confessed to me as we rode on that he had been somewhat "turned about." As for me, I thought that was the most awful country to get "turned about" in I ever saw.

"Whoa, dar! Whoa, dar! Whar you gwine wid dat dar mule o' mine? Whoa, 'Ginger'!"

The mule stopped stock still as we caught sight of the black head and face of a darky boy peering forth from the door of a tobacco-house that we were passing. Possibly he was the owner of the plantation now, and the mule "Ginger" might be his only live stock.

"Where are we going, Sam? Why, we're going on to Raleigh!"

"On ter Raleigh! And wid dat dar mule o' mine? 'Clar to goodness, sodgers, can't git along widout dat mule. Better git off'n dat dar mule!"

"Whip him up, 'Jasper'!" shouted I.

"Come up! Get along, Beauregard!" shouted "Jasper."

And we both laid on quite lustily, but never an inch would that miserable mule budge from the position he had taken on hearing the darky's voice. All of a sudden, and as if a mine had been sprung under our feet, there was such a striking out of heels and such an uncomfortable elevation in the rear, the angle of which was increased, that at last, with an enormous spring, "Jasper" and I were sent flying off into the road.

"Yi! yi! yi! Didn' I say better git off'n dat dar mule o' mine? Yi! yi! yi!"

Laughing as heartily as the darky at our misadventure, we felt that it would be safer to make for the river afoot. We had a glorious plunge in the waters of the Pedee, and returned to the regiment at sundown, greatly refreshed and a good deal cleaner.

March 6: Warm and pleasant. We were compelled to lie over here to bridge the river.

We heard very heavy explosions down the river, in the direction of Cheraw, S. C. The pontoniers worked all night, and by the morning of March 7 the bridge was completed. We crossed at 7 A.M., and marched sixteen miles. 8th: Rained all day. Marched twenty-five miles.

March 9: Marched eighteen miles. It rained all day. This was a terrible day's march. The roads were so muddy and our clothes so wet that it was almost impossible to march, and I was so tired at night that I could barely write, and had partly made up my mind to give up keeping a diary After getting into camp on a day's march like this I was too tired to write much.

March 10: Marched five miles and went into camp to wait for the rest of the army to close up. Weather fair and clear, but the roads were still very heavy.

March 11: Marched thirteen miles to Fayetteville, N. C., where we found an abundance of flour, meal, bacon, molasses, coffee, and tobacco, and lived on the best the country afforded.

Sabbath, March 12: Lay in camp. Everything was quiet. The tug-boat "Donaldson" arrived at Fayetteville from Wilmington with news from Generals Terry and Schofield and returned the same day with despatches from Sherman.

March 13 and 14 were passed by us in Fayetteville. The arsenal and the machinery, which had formerly belonged to the Harper's Ferry arsenal, were completely destroyed. Every building was knocked down and burned, and every piece of machinery broken up and utterly ruined.

March 15: Rainy General Bishop had orders to destroy a large cotton-mill near our camp. The poor people in the neighborhood, who had always worked there, begged to have it saved, as it was their only means of support. Five companies remained as rear guard and to destroy the mill and one other building that was left. The other five companies moved over the Cape Fear River. We marched six miles and encamped. 16th: Cloudy and windy, with rain. We moved along very slowly, making but four miles before going into camp.

March 17: "St. Patrick's day." In honor of the Irishmen of the regiment, the band on the march played nothing but the air of "St. Patrick's Day in the Morning." We marched four miles, crossing the Black River, and encamped on the north bank.

Sunday, March 19: Weather fine. The roads were much better now. The soil was sandy, and absorbed the water as fast as it fell, leaving the roads in good condition.

March 20: Were relieved as rear guard and

ordered to the front. The Fourteenth and Twentieth Corps, under Slocum, fought the battle of Bentonville. Two men of our regiment were wounded. We remained on the field until dark, then fell back in the rear of the second line of our works, and bivouacked. Marched ten miles. 21st: Rained all day. Lay in camp. Orders to prepare to march at a moment's warning. 22d: Broke camp at 7 A.M., but did not move until 4 P.M.; then marched ten miles between that time and 7 P.M. We had nothing to eat, neither bread nor meat. 23d: Windy and disagreeable. Crossed the Neuse River, marched to Goldsboro', and were reviewed by Generals Sherman, Slocum, Howard, and Schofield. Marched eighteen miles.

March 24: Windy but warm. Band serenaded the Eighth Minnesota and Colonel Thomas, also Captain Cilley, who was now on General Schofield's staff. 25th: Warm and windy. The regiment was ordered out six miles from camp, to guard a grist-mill that our men were running, grinding meal for the soldiers.

March 26 to the 31st: We had drilled twice a day and in the evening had dress parade, and, of course, had to do our share of guard and picket duty, which did not give us much time for amusement. A member of the Seventeenth New York Cavalry was to be shot that day by order of General Sherman. The poor fellow who was to suffer the highest penalty of military law was, I was informed, a New York man. The crime for which he was to give his life was rape, committed on an old lady On that bright spring morning orders came to the effect that the whole division of which he was a member was to turn out at one o'clock to witness the execution of the sentence. I need hardly say that this was most unwelcome news. Nobody wished to see so sad a sight. Some of the men begged to be excused from attending, and others could not be found when their drums beat the "assembly;" for none could well endure, as they said, "to see a man shot down like a dog." However, in condescension to this altogether natural and humane aversion to the shedding of blood, and in order to render the task as endurable as possible, the customary practice was observed. On the morning of the execution an officer, who had been appointed for the purpose, took a number of rifles, some twelve or fourteen in number, and loaded all of them carefully with powder and ball except one, which was loaded with powder only. He then mixed the guns so thoroughly that he himself could scarcely tell which guns were loaded with ball and which one was not. Another officer then distributed the guns to the men, not one of whom could be at all certain whether his particular gun contained a ball or not, and all of them could avail themselves of the full benefit of the doubt in the case. At the appointed hour the division marched out and took position in a large field, or clearing, surrounded on all sides by pine woods. They were drawn up so as to occupy three sides of a great hollow square, two ranks deep, facing inward, the fourth side of the square (where I could see a grave had been recently dug) being left open for the execution.

Scarcely were the troops well in position, when there came to my ears, wafted by the sighing spring wind, the mournful notes of the "Dead March." Looking away in the direction whence the music came, I could see a long procession marching sadly and slowly to the measured stroke of the muffled drum. First came the band, playing the dirge; next the squad of executioners; then a pine coffin carried by four men; then the prisoner himself, dressed in his fatigue uniform, and marching in the midst of four guards; then a number of men under arrest for various offences, who had been brought out for the sake of the moral effect it was hoped this spectacle might have upon them. Last of all came a strong guard.

When the procession had come up to the place where the division was formed, and had reached the open side of the hollow square, it wheeled to the left, inside of the line, from the right to the left, the band still playing the dirge. The line was long and the step was slow, and it seemed as if they would never get to the other end. But at last, after having solemnly traversed the entire length of the three sides of the hollow square, the procession came to the open side of it, opposite to the point from which it had started. The escort wheeled off. The prisoner was placed before his coffin, which was set down in front of the grave. The squad of twelve men who were to shoot the unfortunate man took position some twelve yards from the grave, facing the prisoner, and a chaplain stepped out from the group of division officers near by, and prayed with and for the poor fellow a long, long time. Then the bugle sounded. The prisoner, standing proudly erect before his grave, had his eyes bandaged, and calmly folded his arms across his breast The bugle sounded again. The officer in charge of the squad stepped forward; then I heard the command, given as calmly as if on drill, "Ready! Aim!" then, drowning out the third command, "Fire!" came a flash of smoke and a loud report. The surgeons ran up to the spot. The bands and drum-corps of the division struck up a quick step as the division faced to the right and marched past the grave, in order that in the dead form of its occupant they might all see that the doom of the perpetration of such a crime was death. It was a sad sight. As the troops moved along, I could see many a rough fellow, from whom you would hardly have expected any sign of pity, pretending to be adjusting his cap so as to screen his eyes from the glare of the western sun, and furtively drawing his hand across his face and dashing away the tears that could not be kept from trickling down the bronzed and weather-beaten cheek. As they marched off the field I could not help being sensible of the harsh contrast between the lively music to which their feet were keeping time and the fearfully solemn scene I had just witnessed. The transition from the "Dead March" to the quick step was quite too sudden. A deep solemnity pervaded the ranks as they marched homeward across the open field and into the sombre pine woods beyond, thinking, I suppose, as they went of the poor fellow's home somewhere among the pleasant hills of New York State, and of the sad and heavy hearts there would be there when it was known that he had paid the extreme penalty of the law.

April 1: Warm and pleasant. The band played at corps head-quarters at 3 P.M., and at six o'clock we had dress parade. 2d: Warm, with a clear, bright sky. Remained in camp all day. 3d: Cold and cloudy. Major Uline arrived with a number of recruits from Minnesota.

April 4: Cloudy and windy. We serenaded the Fourth Minnesota Regiment; also brigade head-quarters. We stayed here, at Goldsboro', until the morning of April 10, when we broke camp and marched northward twelve miles. The Second Division of our corps skirmished with the Confederates all day. It rained all day, and at 10 P.M. it was still raining.

April 11: Cloudy, but pleasant. We were confronted by the rebels all day; but our brigade drove them steadily back to Smithfield, where we went into camp.

April 12: We marched twelve miles to Clayton, N. C., and crossed the Neuse River. The lieutenant-governor of the State came to General Sherman on a flag-of-truce mission, I understood, to surrender the capital of the State, Raleigh, so there should be no destruction of property.

April 13: Rained all forenoon, but turned out nice in the afternoon. We marched fifteen miles to Raleigh, and found it a very handsome city. We encamped near the Insane Asylum, in the south part of the city.

April 14: Very hot. We marched fourteen miles to Jones's Cross-roads.

April 15: Cloudy and rainy. Our brigade was scattered along the roads with the wagon-train, lifting them out of the mud and making roads. Marched five miles to Chapel Hill College.

April 16: Warm and pleasant. We marched five miles and went into camp. Nothing worthy of note occurred.

April 17: Hot. Remained in camp. Rumors that Johnston had surrendered; but before night we were informed that there was no truth in it.

Tuesday, April 18: Weather pleasant. We heard the sad news of the assassination of President Lincoln. After all of our victories and successful campaigns, and just at the eve of peace, we had lost our commander-in-chief, our much-loved "Old Abe." The dark pall of sorrow hung over the army that day. In all history there never was a national sorrow to be compared to this. Literally, the whole army wept. Thousands there were who would willingly have received the fatal bullet in their own hearts, if thereby they could have saved the life of our precious leader.

> Perished? Who was it said
> Our leader has passed away?
> Dead? Our President dead?
> He has not died for a day.

Ye winds that move over the mighty places of the West chant the requiem. Yes, comrades, behold the martyr whose blood, as so many articulate words, pleads for fidelity, for law, for liberty

April 19: Warm and pleasant. The death of the President was the main topic of conversation. In what way to account for it I know not, but so it is, that soldiers always have been, and, I suppose, always will be, merry-hearted fellows, and full of good spirits. One would naturally suppose that, having so much to do with hardship and danger every day, they would be sober and serious above the generality of men. But such was by no means the case with our regiment. In camp, on the march, nay, even in the solemn hour of battle, there was ever and anon a laugh passing down the line, or some sport going on inside of the tents. Seldom was there wanting some one, noted for his powers of story-telling, to beguile the weary hours about the camp-fire in front of our shelters, or out among the pines on picket. Few companies could be found without some native-born wag or wit, whose comical songs or quaint remarks kept the boys in good humor, while at the same time each and all, according to the measure of their several capacities, were given to playing practical jokes of one kind or other for the general enlivenment of the camp. So the gloom of the President's assassination was gradually forgotten.

We remained at this camp until April 27. The weather had been warm at times, and hot at others, but, take it as a whole, it had been what would be called June weather in Minnesota.

About 2 A.M. we heard on our left heavy cannonading and the rumbling sound of musketry. We were called out in line of battle and remained in this position until sunrise. In the mean time, the thunder of artillery came nearer and nearer, and the troops were getting nervous, for we were expecting our last great battle with Johnston. Suddenly we espied an officer, mounted on a large, fine, white horse, with hat off and waving it over his head, dashing along the line crying, "Johnston has surrendered! Johnston has surrendered, and peace is declared!" At the announcement of this, cheer upon cheer went up. Artillerymen loaded and fired their guns with fixed ammunition as fast as they could. The infantry soon followed suit, and such a roar of musketry and artillery, cheering and hurrahing, will never be heard again.

April 28: Warm and pleasant. With joyful feelings of the news of peace, we broke camp and marched northward ten miles and encamped.

We met on our march the straggling troops of General Lee's army who had surrendered to Grant and were returning South to their homes, while we were on the same road going North to be disbanded. Our boys and the Confederates exchanged jokes as we passed each other. One of our boys said,—

"Well Johnnie, we've got you at last,— knocked out as it were!"

"Oh, yes," replied Johnnie, "but we gave you the best we had in the shop; and another thing, we know when we've got enough. We're no hogs. We would have been home long ago if you had let us."

One poor fellow I was talking to remarked,—

"I reckon Sherman didn't leave us any homes to go to. What are we poor fellows going to do, going back into our country without a dollar in our pocket, our homes destroyed, stock driven away, and our families scattered, God only knows where? Oh, war! it is horrible! horrible!" And the poor fellow cried like a child.

April 29: Warm and pleasant. We marched ten miles to Holly Springs, and got into camp at one o'clock in the afternoon. We turned over to the proper officials all of our government stores, such as extra arms and ammunition, to be stored here until otherwise disposed of by the government.

Sunday, April 30: Peace and happiness reigned over the land. The song-birds in the woods seemed to know it. The weather could not be finer,—balmy and pleasant; the roads were in excellent condition. We marched sixteen miles and crossed Tar River, where we halted to prepare dinner, after which we marched five miles, and encamped three miles south of Oxford Court-House, N. C. We marched in all twenty-four miles.

May 2: Warm. Marched three miles, through Oxford, then fourteen miles to Williamsburg, and five miles north, and encamped for the night; altogether twenty-two miles.

May 3: Warm, with clear, bright sky. Marched fifteen miles and crossed the Roanoke River, over the North Carolina line, into Virginia.

May 4: Marched twenty-five miles, crossed the Meherrin River, and encamped on the north shore.

May 5: Weather hot. Several of our men were sun-struck. We passed through Lunenburg and Nottoway Court-House, marching twenty-three miles in all.

May 6: Hot and sultry. Crossed the Appomattox River. Marched twenty-seven miles to within three miles of Richmond, two miles south of the James River. We remained here until the morning of the 10th. In the mean time, we were allowed passes to go into Richmond. The greater part of the city having been destroyed by fire by General Ewell, of the Confederate army, the grand streets and avenues were strewn with *débris* and plunder of every description. An old gentleman told me that Capitol Square seemed to be the safest place from the conflagration, and it was covered over with piles of furniture dragged from burning buildings; among which were huddled together women and children, whose only homes were now beneath the open sky. Among the beautiful statues that adorned Capitol Square I noticed those of Patrick Henry, Madison, Jefferson, Henry Clay, and an equestrian statue of Washington. I visited the State capitol, the residence of Jeff. Davis, and also that of General Lee, after which we examined Libby Prison and Castle Thunder, of which I made no mention in my diary. I knew that after the war historians would write it up and give a more vivid description of its horrors than I in my humble way could expect to do.

May 11: Marched though Manchester, across the James River, on through Richmond, and were reviewed by General Sherman and our corps commanders. Marched twenty-one miles.

May 12: Very hot. Marched twelve miles,

through Hanover Court-House, across the Pamunkey River, and encamped.

May 13: Warm. Marched twenty-miles. Crossed the Rappahannock at Ellis's Ford, and encamped near a large brick house in the edge of the timber. This was the gold-mining district of Virginia: but, from appearances, I should judge, if there had remained any gold, the Confederate government would have worked the mine to assist them in their lost cause.

May 14: Marched fourteen miles and encamped four miles west of the battle-field of the Wilderness; the country seemed to be uninhabited. The few buildings that remained and were saved from the torch, shot, and shell were vacant and in a dilapidated condition. It would take many years to replace and reconstruct what Virginia had lost during this wicked and cruel war.

May 15: Hot. We marched eighteen miles, crossed the Rapidan at Cedar Mountain, and encamped.

May 16: Marched fifteen miles, forded the Rapidan again, and made preparations to encamp, but were ordered on five miles farther north.

May 17: Marched seventeen miles, forded Bull-Run Creek, and encamped. The weather was very hot and oppressive.

May 18: Weather continued hot. Passed

through Centreville and Fairfax Court-House, and encamped on part of the estate of R. E. Lee.

May 19: Marched eight miles, passed the Lee mansion, which is said to have been erected in early colonial days, and encamped on Arlington Heights, in sight of Washington.

May 20: It seemed as if the dry, hot weather had ended, after our long and dusty march, for the rain came down in torrents, and we were compelled to sit in our little shelter-tents all day

May 21: Still raining; the camp was muddy and everything looked dismal and disagreeable. A sutler came into camp and made things a little lively

May 22: Weather very hot. Had rumors in camp that recruits and drafted men were to be immediately discharged, and the veterans were to be organized into a veteran corps and sent to Mexico. We were not prepared for anything like this. The rebellion was ended and now we thought the government should send us home; and if they had some other project in view, why not try to build up an army out of the disbanded troops of both Sherman's and Grant's two great armies. I thought that in about a month after disbandment there would be thousands who would gladly go into an adventure of that kind.

May 23: The Army of the Potomac was reviewed. Now that the record of blood was written, and the scene of four years' carnage was ended, the soldiers were returning to their homes; and as they passed through the streets they were welcomed back with grateful shouts, —their banners tattered, and their arms and uniforms battle-soiled. Many an absent one was mourned; and the fresh faces which went forth to defend their country returned now, worn with the hardships of war; but they had faithfully served their country, and their steps were justly proud as they marched in triumph through the streets of Washington receiving the plaudits of a grateful nation.

May 24: The armies of Grant and Sherman, who had shared in the last struggle, as they passed through Washington, marshalled in review over two hundred thousand strong, making a grand spectacle. They were assembled in one body for the first time. They were gathered together from every battle-field of the Union, from the Ohio to New Orleans, from New Orleans to Charleston, from Charleston to the Appomattox.

Those who looked upon this spectacle were reminded of the first stages of the war, when the national capital was threatened and when the first recruits rushed to its rescue. They looked upon a living, moving demonstration of the fact that treason in a republic could be subdued, though every rebel leader, from Davis and Stephens down to the most petty demagogue of the South, had prophesied to the contrary

There was something to mar the triumph. A general who had marched and fought his army from Chattanooga, through the fortifications of Atlanta, to the sea, thence to Goldsboro' and Washington, still felt the wrong which had been studiously thrust upon him by some officers of the government. Sherman could not shake hands with Halleck. We also grievously missed the presence of Lincoln, who had called us to conflict, and whom we had always looked upon as a father and friend.

But may we not believe that Lincoln, though withdrawn from earth, looked down upon this sublime spectacle? Did he not, as one of our poets imagined, marshal another host, composed of those who, like him, had been victims of this Civil War, and who participated in this last grand review.

We marched down Pennsylvania Avenue, on which every house was beautifully decorated, with bunting, streamers, and flags flying from every window and house-top. The people were wild with enthusiasm. With one accord the nation turned towards its armies and showered its blessings upon them.

We passed through Washington, over Georgetown Heights, to the aqueduct, through which we marched to the south shore of the Potomac to our camp. Our march in review was twelve miles.

May 25: Weather warm and pleasant. Broke camp at 8 A.M., and marched across the long bridge over the Potomac, through Washington, and encamped two miles north of the city. We remained at this camp until June 14. In the mean time, regiment after regiment had gone home and been discharged. I had taken in all the sights in and about Washington City, such as the Capitol, Treasury Building, White House, Smithsonian Institution, Patent-Office, and Navy-Yard. I went down the Potomac to Mount Vernon and visited the tomb of Washington, and spent half a day looking over those beautiful grounds.

June 14: It had been for the last two or three weeks hot and dry, not enough moisture to lay the dust; but as we were about to start for the West, loaded on open coal-cars with rough board benches for seats, the rain poured down in torrents.

June 15: Passed through Harper's Ferry, Martinsburg, and Cumberland. At the last-named place we stopped for a short time to get coffee, pork, and beans, which were furnished by the citizens. The coffee was in barrels, nice and hot. We soon satisfied our appetites, and again, in our muddy and filthy cars, proceeded on our way. It would be well to say something about these cars. They were made to haul coal in; had sides from eighteen inches to two feet high, and were perfectly water-tight. After the hard rain of the previous day and night there was in the neighborhood of six inches of dirty black water in each car, in which our feet hung soaking. When the train ascended a grade, the water would come back with a rush and dash over the rear end of the car, and *vice versa* when we went down grade. After arriving at Cumberland we procured axes and knocked out a few boards from the bottom of the cars; after which we had a little more comfort.

This was one of the rare cases where we travelled by land and water at the same time.

On the afternoon of the 16th we arrived at Parkersburg, W. Va., and went into camp near an oil refinery, where we lay until 11.30 on the 17th, when we embarked on transports and proceeded down the Ohio River. 18th: Still on the river, enjoying ourselves the best we knew how. 19th: Arrived at Louisville, Ky., and marched out on the Munfordville Pike, where we went into camp. We remained at Louisville until July 11. In the mean time, we had done no duty of any kind, except occasionally a dress parade. The following order was read on parade, which fully set at rest all the rumors that we were to do garrison duty in the South for another year:

"HEAD-QUARTERS FOURTEENTH ARMY CORPS,
"LOUISVILLE, KY., July 9, 1865.

"GENERAL J. W. BISHOP:

"I have the honor to enclose to you a copy of the order relieving your regiment from the corps, and directing you to report it at Fort Snelling.

"Until the time of separation came none knew how strong were the attachments formed in our months and years of associations in hardships and dangers as soldiers. His relations to the officers and men of the Second Minnesota have always been a matter of pride and satisfaction to the corps commander, and from no regiment in the corps will he part with a deeper regret.

"He thanks one and all of the members of the organization for the constancy and devotion which have always marked their attention to the duties and requirements of soldiers in camp and on the march, as well as on the field of action.

"He congratulates you that your labors, hardships, and dangers are over, and that, with a country restored to peace and prosperity, partly through your exertions and sacrifices, you return once more to your homes.

"None have a better record for discipline and drill and all the minutiæ of soldierly conduct as well as uniform gallantry on every field of action in which they have been engaged than the Second Minnesota; and your State owes you thanks for the uniformly faithful manner in which you have performed your share of the task allotted to the soldiers of the Union.

"Very Respectfully,
"Your Most Obedient Servant,
A. C. McCLURG,
"*Brevet Colonel, A.A.G., and Chief of Staff.*"

Tuesday July 11: We crossed the Ohio River to Jeffersonville, and took transportation on the Michigan Central Railroad for Chicago, where we arrived on the evening of the 13th. Remained over night, and on the morning of the 14th proceeded on our way over the Chicago and North-Western Railroad to La Crosse, where we arrived on the 15th, and were immediately marched on board the steamer "McLellan," and proceeded up the Mississippi River. As we came around the bend below St. Paul, on the morning of the 16th, we saw great crowds of people on the levee who were waiting to welcome us.

At last we landed, amid booming of cannon and the cheering of multitudes of people. Bells were rung, people paraded the streets, to welcome us home, and everybody was glad beyond a possibility of expression.

And among the joyful thousands all over the land, the "Boys in Blue" were probably the gladdest of all; for the war was over, and "Johnny came marching home" to see the girl he had left behind him. We marched up Third Street to Wabashan Street, thence to the State capitol, where we partook of a bounteous collation, to which we did ample justice. One old darky, who was passing coffee around, remarked, "Dem sodjers dar must be done gone starved, dat's sartin. Nebber seen sech hungry men in all my bawn days,—nebber!"

After dinner we marched to the upper landing and again boarded the steamboat, and started for Fort Snelling, where we remained, awaiting our pay and discharges, which were completed on Thursday, July 20.

We were then disbanded and said the last "good-by" to our comrades in arms, the great majority of whom we would never, in all probability, see again. And a more hearty, rough-

and-ready, affectionate good-by there never was in all this wide world. Songs were sung, hands were shaken, or rather rung, many a loud, hearty "God bless you, old fellow!" resounded, and many were the toasts and the healths that were drunk before the men parted for good.

It was midnight when the last camp-fire of the old Second Minnesota Regiment broke up. "Good-by, boys; good-by! God bless you old fellow!" was shouted again and again, as by companies or in squads we were off for our different homes, some of us bound north, some east, some west, but, thank God! all bound for "Home, sweet Home!"

PEACE.

Oh, fairest land beneath the sun,
    A golden glory fills the air,
And drives the battle vapor dim
    Away from hills and valleys fair.

The cannon's throbbing notes are still;
    We hear no more the rifle's crack;
And blackly dotting all the hill,
    We see no army's bloody track.

The drums are hushed, the air is still
    Of all the direful sounds of war;
And peace is blending on the hill,
    And sends the greeting smile afar.

The battle-flags are furled away,
  No more to flutter in the light;
What need have we of them to-day?
  The wrong lies prone before the right.

No more along the throbbing wires
  Come bitter tidings of the fray;
But on the hills the victor's fires
  Light up the dawn of freedom's day.

Oh, nation long the starless night;
  But now, along the clearing sky,
The morning breaks with peaceful light,
  And sees the battle's shadows die.

In this glad hour, join heart and hand;
  No blot should mar this golden day,
Or cast a shadow o'er the land,
  From which the night has passed away.

Send upward through the listening air
  One universal psalm of praise;
To heaven and Him, who reigneth there,
  Our grateful hearts to-day we raise.

And while we chant the victory hymn
  A thought steals in upon our souls;
And, spite of all, our eyes grow dim,
  And voices lose their stern control.

We think of those who died that they
  Might make the nation great and free:
They won the "Peace" we know to-day,
  This grand and bless<i>é</i>d liberty.

Fame writes to-day upon our rolls
  The deeds that make our land sublime;
And chant a requiem for their souls,
  Of those whose names belong to time,

Give us thy benediction, peace;
  Drop blessings on our chastened land;
From North to South, and West to East,
  Walk thou with freedom hand in hand.

THE END.

www.ingramcontent.com/pod-product-compliance
Lightning Source LLC
Chambersburg PA
CBHW031817220426
43662CB00007B/690